The
Money Men

Beneath the surface of business affairs lies the drama of human affairs. In the Atlas Books–W. W. Norton Enterprise series, distinguished writers tell the stories of the dynamic innovators and the compelling ideas that create new institutions, new ways of doing business and creating wealth, even new societies. Intended for both business professionals and the general reader, these are books whose insights come from the realm of business but inform the world we live in today.

The Money Men: Capitalism, Democracy, and the Hundred Years' War Over the American Dollar

Andrew Jackson: His Life and Times

Lone Star Nation: The Epic Story of the Battle for Texas Independence

Woodrow Wilson

The Age of Gold: The California Gold Rush and the New American Dream

The Strange Death of American Liberalism

The First American: The Life and Times of Benjamin Franklin

Masters of Enterprise: Giants of American Business from John Jacob Astor and J. P. Morgan to Bill Gates and Oprah Winfrey

What America Owes the World: The Struggle for the Soul of Foreign Policy

TR: The Last Romantic

The Reckless Decade: America in the 1890s

Since Vietnam: The United States in World Affairs, 1973– 1995

The Wages of Globalism: Lyndon Johnson and the Limits of American Power

The United States in the World: A History of American Foreign Relations

Into the Labyrinth: The United States and the Middle East, 1945–1993

The Devil We Knew: Americans and the Cold War

Bound to Empire: The United States and the Philippines

Inside the Cold War: Loy Henderson and the Rise of the American Empire, 1918–1961

India and the United States: The Cold Peace

The Specter of Neutralism: The United States and the Emergence of the Third World, 1947–1960

Cold Warriors: Eisenhower's Generation and American Foreign Policy

The Money Men

Capitalism, Democracy, and the Hundred Years'
War Over the American Dollar

H. W. Brands

Atlas Books

W. W. Norton & Company
New York • London

For information about permission to reproduce selections from this book,
write to Permissions, W. W. Norton & Company, Inc.,
500 Fifth Avenue, New York, NY 10110

Manufacturing by Courier Westford
Book design by Chris Welch
Production manager: Amanda Morrison

Library of Congress Cataloging-in-Publication Data

Brands, H. W.
The money men : capitalism, democracy, and the hundred years' war over
the American dollar / H.W. Brands. — 1st ed.
p. cm. — (Enterprise)
"Atlas Books."
Includes bibliographical references and index.
ISBN-13: 978-0-393-06184-0 (hardcover)
ISBN-10: 0-393-06184-1 (hardcover)
1. Capitalists and financiers—United States—History. 2. Finance—United States—
History. I. Title. II. Series: Enterprise (New York, N.Y.)
HG181.B82 2006
332.092'273—dc22
2006009919

ISBN 978-0-393-33050-2 pbk.

W. W. Norton & Company, Inc.
500 Fifth Avenue, New York, N.Y. 10110
www.wwnorton.com

W. W. Norton & Company Ltd.
15 Carlisle Street, London W1D 3BS

3 4 5 6 7 8 9 0

Contents

The
Money Men

Prologue
The Money Question

For the first five generations of America's independent history—from 1776 till the eve of World War I—a single question vexed American politics and the American economy more persistently than any other. Political careers were made and broken on this question; political parties rose and fell. Great wealth rewarded those who answered it correctly; bankruptcy claimed those who got it wrong. No question touched more livelihoods and more lives more consistently, more intimately, more portentously.

The question was the money question. In simplest form it asked: What constitutes money in the United States? Gold? Silver? Paper currency? Bank notes? Checks? This central question raised subsidiary questions. How much money shall there be? Who ought to control it? To what ends?

The money question has been a puzzle for every society since the first ancient hit on the idea of employing proxies—seashells, shiny rocks, rare metals—for value. But it was a particular conundrum for the United States during the eighteenth, nineteenth, and early twentieth centuries. This period encompassed the emergence of the two institutions that made modern America what it is today: democracy and capitalism. From the start an inherent tension existed between the two. The driving force of democracy is equality, of capitalism inequality. Democratic equality begins in the political sphere but bleeds into the economic realm; capitalist inequality arises in the marketplace but encroaches upon the public square.

The money question lay at the center of the contest between democracy and capitalism. The democrats demanded that the people control the money supply, to preserve and extend equality. Money was too important to everyday lives to be left to self-interested capitalists. The capitalists countered that managing money was a talent given to few, that even if the democrats were well-meaning (a dubious premise, in many capitalist minds), their inexpertise would doom their efforts and destabilize the economy. Besides, money was property, and property needed protecting from the masses.

Had the two groups—the democrats and the capitalists—been distinct, their struggle over money would have been bitter and trying enough. But in America the two groups overlapped substantially. By the middle of the nineteenth century only the archest of capitalists could gainsay democracy, at least in theory. And most American democrats were capitalists themselves, prospective capitalists, or dependent on capitalists in one way or another. In his first inaugural address, after a brutal campaign fought over the money question, among others, Thomas Jefferson declared, "We are all Federalists, we are all Republicans." Jefferson's listeners knew the Federalists as the party of emerging capitalism, the Republicans as the party of nascent democracy. And they might have extrapolated his dictum to the money question and concluded, correctly, that in a fundamental sense Americans were all capitalists and all democrats. But Americans had difficulty keeping their identities straight, with the result that policies and attitudes toward money careened wildly. Capitalism charted the course for a time, then democracy, then capitalism, then democracy.

The stormy seas of finance were no place for the faint of heart, but to the intrepid they offered unparalleled opportunities to serve the cause of democracy and the imperatives of capitalism— sometimes separately, sometimes together. In every generation a few such bold spirits stood out, grappling with the question on which the fate of the American political economy hung. They were geniuses and rascals, statesmen and speculators, patriots and profiteers. They were the Money Men.

1

The Aristocracy of Capital

Alexander Hamilton had been impatient his whole life. As a boy on the Caribbean island of Nevis he ached to escape the stigma of his illegitimate birth. As a thirteen-year-old clerk in St. Croix, he couldn't wait to find something better. "I contemn the groveling and condition of a clerk or the like, to which my fortune etc. condemns me," he wrote a friend. "I wish there was a war." St. Croix taught Hamilton about money and trade. At the crossroads of three empires—the British, French, and Spanish—he dealt in rum and cod and bread and mules, denominated in pounds and livres and dollars, backed by gold and silver and land and promises. But there was rarely enough of any currency so far from the imperial metropoles. "I am a good deal puzzled to fulfill your engagements," he wrote his employer when the latter was away. "Cash is scarce."

It remained scarce after Hamilton escaped the West Indies for New York. His break followed a 1772 hurricane that ravaged St. Croix but allowed the clever young man to gain the ear of the world by penning a graphic account of the storm that was printed in several papers. "Good God! What horror and destruction. . . . It seemed as if a total dissolution of nature was taking place. The roaring of the sea and wind, fiery meteors flying about in the air, the prodigious glare of almost perpetual lightning, the crash of falling houses, and ear-piercing shrieks of the distressed, were sufficient to strike astonishment into Angels." Perhaps it was the vividness of his portrayal that arrested readers' attention, perhaps the devotional gloss he appended. "Where now, oh vile worm, is all thy boasted fortitude and resolution?" he asked of humanity. "See thy wretched, helpless state. . . . Despise thyself, and adore thy God." Or perhaps it was his capacity for flattering those in power. "Our General has issued several very salutary and humane regulations, and both in his public and private measures has shewn himself *the Man*." Whatever the cause, a group of benefactors decided the boy was meant for better things and sent him to New York for an education.

Hamilton hurried through King's College, soon rechristened Columbia on account of the troubles that developed between King George and his American subjects. Hamilton embraced the troublemakers. "That Americans are entitled to freedom is incontestable upon every rational principle," he declared. He enthusiastically endorsed attempts to hit the British where it hurt the most: in the commerce that connected the American colonies to the motherland. "This commerce Great Britain has hitherto regulated to her own advantage. Can we think the annihilation of so exuberant a source of wealth a matter of trifling import? On the contrary, must it not be productive of the most disastrous

(margin handwritten note: trade = important for G.B.)

effects?" As he would the rest of his life, Hamilton contended that economics ruled the world, eventually if not at once. The American colonies had been planted as a commercial venture; if the venture proved unprofitable—as a boycott of British commerce would render it—then the colonies' British sponsors would feel the pain. A boycott would bring Britain's commercial classes to their knees and consequently Britain's government to its senses.

But economics acted too slowly for some of the colonists; the boycott acquired martial assistance when fighting broke out in April 1775 at Lexington and Concord between American militia and British regulars. The Continental Congress appointed George Washington, America's most experienced officer, to head up the Continental Army and oppose the British outside Boston. Hamilton contributed from the distance of Manhattan. He harangued his classmates in favor of the rebel cause, aided in the rescue of cannons at the Battery from capture by the British, and organized an artillery company of volunteers, with himself as captain. He fought in the unsuccessful defense of New York (made more difficult by the pro-British influence of the city's large number of Loyalists) and in Washington's retreat across New Jersey. His valor and abilities won the esteem of his superiors, of whom two offered to make him aide-de-camp. He declined, claiming disdain for the "personal dependence" such a staff position entailed. In fact he was holding out for better, and when Washington requested that Hamilton join his entourage he accepted at once.

The young man—he was either twenty or twenty-two; the

date of his bastard birth has long provoked dispute—didn't cut an imposing figure. A fellow officer recalled his first sight of Hamilton. "I noticed a youth, a mere stripling, small, slender, almost delicate in frame, marching beside a piece of artillery with a cocked hat pulled down over his eyes, apparently lost in thought, with his hand resting on the cannon and every now and then patting it as he mused, as if it were a favorite horse or a pet plaything." Yet Hamilton's restless ambition soon won him ascendance over the other junior officers on Washington's staff. He learned to anticipate his superior's wishes and to supply them better than anyone else, till he became Washington's de facto chief of staff.

He shared Washington's frustration at the failure of America's legislators to supply basic provisions for the army. "Folly, caprice, a want of foresight, comprehension and dignity, characterise the general tenor of their actions," he scribbled with frozen fingers from the windswept hillside of Valley Forge. "Their conduct with respect to the army especially is feeble, indecisive, and improvident." The troops went naked for lack of uniforms; they grew hungry, sick, and mutinous. Many deserted. Hamilton blamed the lawmakers but also the configuration of the American government, which left sovereignty to the states. "Each State, in order to promote its own internal government and prosperity, has selected its best members to fill the offices within itself." The second-raters found positions in the Continental Congress, where they looked out for their states first. "Local attachment, falsely operating, has made them more provident for the particular interests of the states. . . . It is necessary there should be a change. America will shake to its center if there is not."

Armies in those days took winters off from fighting. Hamilton had time to visit friends and court the ladies. He developed decided tastes in the latter, as he did in most things. "She must be young, handsome (I lay most stress upon a good shape)," he wrote regarding his ideal woman, "sensible (a little learning will do), well bred (but she must have an aversion to the word *ton*), chaste and tender (I am an enthusiast in my notions of fidelity and fondness), of some good nature, a great deal of generosity (she must neither love money nor scolding, for I dislike equally a termagant and an economist)." Her politics didn't matter. "I think I have arguments that will easily convert her to mine." She ought to be Christian but not Catholic. As to money in hand: "The larger stock of that the better. Money is an essential ingredient to happiness in this world. . . . As I have not much of my own, and as I am very little calculated to get more either by my address or industry, it must needs be that my wife, if I get one, bring at least a sufficiency to administer to her own extravagances."

Elizabeth Schuyler met most of Hamilton's specifications, possessing warm brown eyes, an appealing figure, and a very wealthy father. The couple were wed in December 1780.

THE MATCH SOLVED Hamilton's money problems but did nothing for those of America. Money had been at the heart of the troubles that provoked the American Revolution, with the colonists resenting and then resisting British taxes not simply on

mercantilism

principle but because they sucked precious specie across the
Atlantic. The colonial policy of the British government reflected
the prevailing mercantilist notion that wealth consisted of gold
and silver and that these must be hoarded in the home country.
The consequence was colonial starvation for money. British
coins—rare gold guineas, somewhat less scarce silver pounds and
shillings—traded at a premium, supplemented by more-numer-
ous Spanish dollars stamped from silver mined in Mexico and
Peru. But even with the Spanish money there were never enough

col. currency

coins, and the colonists resorted to Indian wampum (strings of
shells or beads), "country money" (claims to tobacco, rice, other
crops, or land), and finally paper notes issued by the colonial gov-
ernments. But the British frowned on the paper issues as inflationary and in the 1760s outlawed paper money entirely. The edgy
colonials soon went over the edge into revolution.

The war aggravated the money problems. Trade shriveled
under the British blockade, cutting the supply of specie still further. The newly independent states and the Continental
Congress issued paper notes, but because nothing substantial
supported most of these notes, they rapidly depreciated, adding
the bitter phrase "not worth a Continental" to the lexicon of
wartime experience. French aid to the rebels eventually included
millions of French livres—paper money backed at least nomi-
nally by gold—but these funds were spent chiefly in Europe on
ships, arms, and other supplies and did little to ease the cash crisis in America. (In part as a result of the aid to America, the
French government of Louis XVI had difficulty maintaining the
livre at par with gold; the resulting economic distress hastened

the French Revolution.)

———————

ALEXANDER HAMILTON OBSERVED the money troubles from
ground level in George Washington's army and grew increasingly
irked. "The fundamental defect is a want of power in Congress,"
he asserted. The states had too much power, the central government too little. The states made laws to suit themselves, with
scant concern for the country as a whole. The states meddled in
the affairs of the army, to the detriment of military efficiency.
Most fatally, the states controlled the nation's finances, through
their refusal to cede the power of taxation. "Without certain revenues, a government can have no power," Hamilton declared.
"That power which holds the purse strings absolutely, must rule."

Hamilton proposed a drastic restructuring of the American
government. Congress should have "complete sovereignty in all
that relates to war, peace, trade, finance, and to the management
of foreign affairs." Finance was critical. Congress must have control of "coining money, establishing banks on such terms and
with such privileges as they think proper, appropriating funds
and doing whatever else relates to the operation of finance." On
the income side, the central government must assure itself of
"perpetual revenues, productive and easy of collection, a land
tax, poll tax or the like, which together with the duties on trade
and the unlocated lands would give Congress a substantial existence and a stable foundation for their schemes of finance."

A national, central bank was essential. Before long Hamilton
would become America's leading authority on banking, but at
this time he knew the subject only through his study of history

and his attention to the affairs of other countries. Yet everything he read convinced him that a national bank, privately owned but chartered by the central government and privileged to handle the government's accounts, would make good things easier and bad things less likely. Congress was funding the war through the sale of bonds and the issue of paper money. The bond sales were limited by the patriotism of Americans and the optimism of foreigners; the paper issues were limited by nothing save the supply of rags that made the notes. The result was the ruinous inflation that impoverished the people and defeated the purpose of the paper.

A national bank was the answer. Such a bank could float loans in the form of notes that would circulate as currency, but the extent of the loans would depend on the solid assets—chiefly gold and silver—at the bank's disposal. Hamilton believed bankers were more circumspect than politicians, yet he didn't depend on the bankers' circumspection for the success of his scheme. Their self-interest in preserving the liquidity of the bank would prevent their overreaching. Moreover—and here Hamilton hit a point that would become fundamental to his thinking—a bank would tie the interests of capital to the future of the republic. Under present conditions, capital and the people who controlled it wanted nothing to do with the government's version of money, which depreciated before their eyes. A national bank would draw them out, and draw them in. "The only certain manner to obtain a permanent paper credit is to engage the monied interest immediately in it by making them contribute the whole or part of the stock"—of the bank—"and giving them the whole or part of the profits."

<hr>

AMERICA WASN'T READY for Hamilton's reorganization of government, and it certainly wasn't ready for his bank. The country had all it could do to win the war. France had joined the American cause after the rebels' first major victory, at Saratoga, but the American cause suffered a grievous blow when General Benedict Arnold defected. Hamilton was present at an interview between Arnold's wife and Washington just after the treason became known. "It was the most affecting scene I was ever witness to," he wrote Elizabeth. "All the sweetness of beauty, all the loveliness of innocence, all the tenderness of a wife and all the fondness of a mother"—Mrs. Arnold brought her infant to the interview—"showed themselves in her appearance and conduct. We have every reason to believe she was entirely unacquainted with the plan."

Events soon proved that Mrs. Arnold was a better actor than Hamilton was a judge of character; she had been involved in her husband's plot from the beginning. Hamilton's embarrassment amplified a touchiness that had begun to infect his relations with Washington. Hamilton admired Washington, after a fashion, but he never warmed to him personally. This wasn't surprising, as Washington was famously aloof. But it bothered Hamilton, who anyway had begun to chafe at being a mere staffer when other officers were receiving battle commands. "For three years past, I have felt no friendship for him and have professed none," he wrote his father-in-law in early 1781 regarding Washington. This same letter told that Hamilton had resigned his position on

Washington's staff. The precipitant was an outburst by Washington after Hamilton had arrived unavoidably late for a meeting. "Colonel Hamilton, you have kept me waiting at the head of the stairs these ten minutes," Hamilton said Washington had said. "I must tell you, sir, you treat me with disrespect." Hamilton had been looking for an occasion to quit, and now he had it. "I replied without petulancy but with decision. 'I am not conscious of it, sir, but since you have thought it necessary to tell me so, we part.'" Washington later attempted to mend the breach, but Hamilton stood fast. "Proposals of accommodation have been made on his part but rejected," he informed a friend. "I pledge my honor to you that he will find me inflexible. He shall for once at least repent his ill-humour."

Washington did repent of his ill humor, but Hamilton repented of his own rashness as he searched for a battle command without luck. For months he wrote letters and entreated those who could help him get to the front. An offer came through only as the final campaign of the war took shape in the late summer of 1781. Hamilton received command of a battalion of New York infantry and was ordered to reinforce Washington in Virginia, where the American general had cornered his British counterpart, Lord Cornwallis. Hamilton initially avoided Washington, instead seeking out the Marquis de Lafayette, whom he had met earlier and who now commanded the large French contingent fighting beside the Americans. Lafayette forwarded to Washington's headquarters Hamilton's request that his battalion be thrown into the thick of the fight, but the request languished till Hamilton made a personal appeal to his old superior. Washington couldn't resist, letting Hamilton lead a charge against a British redoubt outside Yorktown. He performed gallantly, inspiring the men by his forward example, and captured the position with modest casualties.

THE END OF the fighting—though not, technically, of the war, which lasted till the signing and ratification of the Treaty of Paris of 1783—forced Hamilton to find other outlets for his ambition. Elizabeth's wealth freed him from mundane matters of livelihood and let him concentrate on winning fame. Politics beckoned, for the troubles that had vexed the nation during the fighting persisted. Hamilton's critique of the structure of American government was no secret; while trolling for his field command he had written a series of pamphlets articulating his views. "The Continentalist," as he called the series, piled case upon case to show that the source of America's problems was "A WANT OF POWER IN CONGRESS." Hamilton reiterated his earlier suggestions for remedies, returning again and again to the essential matter of finance. Congress must have the authority to levy taxes and thereby control its own fate. "Power without revenue in political society is a name," he said dismissively.

Before the series concluded, Hamilton had been elected to Congress from New York. Under the Articles of Confederation, Congress was a unicameral affair, and Hamilton sat with every other member. The towering figures of the Founding had left Congress for assignments in the army (Washington), overseas (Benjamin Franklin, John Adams), or in the states (Thomas

Jefferson). But a second generation was emerging, led by James
Madison, a small man with a large head for constitutional theory.
"He always comes forward the best informed man of any point in
debate," a contemporary remarked of Madison. Hamilton and
Madison discovered they had much in common, including discouragement over the present direction of American affairs and
a desire to alter it.

Alliances aside, Hamilton's congressional service was brief
and frustrating. He spoke repeatedly of the necessity for revenues, but his words produced no effect. The negative highlight
of his tenure revealed the dismal condition of the country's
finances. In June 1783 an angry band of Continental Army soldiers who hadn't been paid in months surrounded the
Philadelphia hall where Congress was meeting. They didn't
exactly threaten mayhem against the delegates, but the latter got
the point. Hamilton hoped the unrest could be turned to
account. "I have myself urged in Congress the propriety of unit-
ing the influence of the public creditors"—who likewise hadn't
been paid—"and the army as part of them, to prevail upon the
states to enter into their views," he wrote Washington. Yet
Hamilton realized he was playing with gunpowder. "As to any
combination of *force,* it would only be productive of the horrors
of a civil war, might end in the ruin of the Country and would
certainly end in the ruin of the army."

The near mutiny convinced Hamilton that the current system
of government was hopeless. He drafted a resolution calling for
a convention to revise the Articles of Confederation, but never
found the right moment to introduce it. He left Congress shortly

thereafter to study law. In 1784 Robert Morris, who had read
Hamilton's plan for a national bank, proposed to create a Bank of
New York and asked Hamilton to draft its charter. Hamilton did
so in exchange for a seat on the bank's board of directors. Upon
his admission to the New York bar he represented some of the
state's wealthiest individuals, including former Loyalists suing to
retrieve property confiscated during the Revolution. His skill at
pleading their cases earned him substantial income but also the
beginning of a reputation as an Anglophile, despite his own service in the cause of independence.

Amid his turn to private affairs, Hamilton never lost sight of
public matters, and when Madison persuaded the Virginia legislature to suggest a convention at Annapolis to address problems
of trade among the several states, Hamilton voiced his support.
The New York assembly sent him to Annapolis, in September
1786, as part of New York's delegation. But almost no one else
showed up. A less resourceful man might have let the apathy dis-
courage him, yet Hamilton simply raised the stakes. He declared
the Annapolis meeting a success and, on behalf of the delegates,
issued a call for a larger convention "to devise such further provisions as shall appear to them necessary to render the constitution of the Federal Government adequate to the exigencies of the
Union." The convention would be held in Philadelphia beginning
in May 1787.

HAMILTON WENT ON to say that any changes to the Articles
devised at Philadelphia would be submitted to Congress for

adoption by the formal process of amendment. He may have been sincere at the time of writing, or only tactically discreet, but events of the next several months convinced him that something more radical than revising the Articles was required. In the 1780s the American economy rested on the twin pillars of agriculture and trade (manufacturing was minuscule as yet). Agriculture employed far more people than trade, but trade was better represented in the state legislatures, on account of the deeper pockets of the merchants, their proximity to the seats of power, and restrictions on voting that still kept most commoners from the polls. The merchants, many being creditors, supported a stronger currency—one that drove prices down and thereby enhanced the value of the debts they were owed. The farmers, most being debtors, analogously wanted a weaker currency and the inflation it entailed. The merchants won out and in several states imposed deflationary policies.

Farmers suffered, and the farmers of western Massachusetts suffered especially. To retire its war debt Massachusetts approved a land tax that shifted the tax burden from the merchant class to farmers, who were already hurting from the falling prices for their crops. The farmers complained, but the state legislature ignored the complaints. The farmers then demanded stay laws to prevent the seizure of their farms for nonpayment of debts. When the legislature rejected this too, the farmers took matters into their own battle-tested hands. Daniel Shays led hundreds of other Revolutionary War veterans against the courts of western Massachusetts and forcibly suspended foreclosures and the prosecution of debtors.

Shays and his fellow rebels cast their actions in the spirit of
the Boston Tea Party and the other resistance to British oppression, and many farmers and debtors elsewhere sympathized. But
merchants and their spokesmen condemned the uprising as sedition. The governor of Massachusetts, James Bowdoin, warned
that the rebellion could produce the "most fatal and pernicious
consequences," including "universal riot, anarchy, and confusion,
which would probably terminate in absolute despotism."
Bowdoin sent the Massachusetts militia against Shays's column.
Yet the Shays men refused to back down, and in fact threatened
to seize the federal arsenal at Springfield. This forced the hand
of Congress, which directed General Henry Knox to raise an
army for use against the rebels. Even George Washington, who
didn't alarm easily, thought conditions had reached a dire pass.
"Good God!" he wrote Knox. "We are far gone in everything igno-
ble and bad. . . . There are combustibles in every state, which a
spark may set fire to."

The Shays rebellion seemed to confirm everything Hamilton
and others had been saying about the need for a stronger central government, one that could deal with uprisings like that in
Massachusetts but also with the financial turmoil that had
produced it. Merely amending the Articles of Confederation
wouldn't do. "The present system neither has nor deserves
advocates," James Madison wrote as he prepared for the
Philadelphia convention.

A majority of the delegates agreed, especially after Rhode
Island boycotted the convention, effectively vetoing, under the
Articles' requirement of unanimity, any amendments. Madison

arrived with a plan for a new government based on representa-
tion by population and specifying election of the executive by the
legislature. The Madison—or Virginia—plan's representational
scheme contrasted sharply with that of the Articles, in which
each state had a single vote, and it favored, to no one's surprise,
large states like Virginia. William Paterson of New Jersey countered with a plan that preserved the one-state, one-vote rule but
greatly expanded the powers of Congress over taxes and trade.

Hamilton declared himself "unfriendly to both plans." The
New Jersey plan allowed the states excessive freedom; the
Virginia plan failed by making the executive answerable to
Congress and thereby to the people. Hamilton believed that the
current crisis demanded the creation of the strongest possible
central government, which in turn required both that the central
government gain power relative to the states and that the
national executive be free of popular restraint. "You cannot have
a good executive upon a democratic plan," he declared. Hamilton
went so far as to recommend the British monarchy as a model.
"See the excellency of the British executive"—which was to say,
the king. "He is placed above temptation. He can have no distinct interests from the public welfare. Nothing short of such an
executive can be efficient." The American executive should be
elected for life. "It may be said this constitutes an elective
monarchy. Pray, what is a monarchy?" Men might quibble over
names, but an energetic, independent executive was essential to
cure the people "of their fondness for democracies."

Hamilton's forthrightness limited his influence at the convention. When Benjamin Franklin suggested opening each session

with a prayer requesting divine guidance, Hamilton reportedly answered that the convention did not require foreign assistance. The Franklin motion was tabled. On another occasion Hamilton won points but no friends. Several delegates were commenting on the aloofness of Washington, the convention's president. Gouverneur Morris, an affable fellow, suggested that the others simply didn't know how to approach the general. Hamilton dared him to act on this opinion. "If you will, at the next reception," Hamilton told Morris, "gently slap him on the shoulder and say, 'My dear General, how happy I am to see you look so well!' a supper and wine shall be provided for you and a dozen of your friends." Morris accepted the dare and the next night did just as Hamilton required. Washington responded by removing Morris's hand from his shoulder and transfixing him with an icy glare. The entire room froze in silence. Hamilton paid up, yet at the dinner Morris declared, "I have won the bet, but paid dearly for it, and nothing could induce me to repeat it."

Midway through the convention Hamilton worried that the whole effort was for naught. The delegates were mired in details. "I am seriously and deeply distressed," he told Washington. "I fear that we shall let slip the golden opportunity of rescuing the American empire from disunion, anarchy, and misery."

The final document was a pleasant surprise. Balancing, in the bicameral Congress, the interests of the small states against the large, it made the executive—the president—independent of the legislature, albeit for four years at a time rather than for life. It also gave Congress crucial powers of finance: to levy taxes and tariffs, to borrow money on the credit of the United States, to pay the public debt, to coin money and regulate its value. And it denied certain financial and economic powers—to coin money, to issue paper notes, to interfere with domestic commerce—to the states.

HAMILTON ENDORSED THE draft constitution and thought it would appeal to those elements of society whose support he considered crucial to the success of any government: the "commercial interest . . . which will give all its efforts to the establishing of a government capable of regulating and the extending the commerce of the Union," the "men of property . . . who wish a government of the Union able to protect them against domestic violence and the depredations which the democratic spirit is apt to make on property," and the "creditors of the United States" who desired a government "able to pay the debt of the Union."

Yet against each of Hamilton's groups was arrayed another group likely to oppose the new Constitution. Farmers distrusted the merchant class; men with little property would oppose what benefited those with much; the original owners of bonds looked askance at paying second owners par value for securities acquired at cents on the dollar.

To tip the balance in favor of ratification, Hamilton proposed the writing of a series of essays explaining the benefits of the new system. He enlisted Madison and John Jay to join him; the result of their labors was the eighty-five-part collection called *The Federalist.* Hamilton wrote most of the essays himself, in a tone that appealed to readers' rational self-interest. "A man must be far gone in Utopian speculations," he said, who couldn't see the necessity of a strong central government. Central control of the nation's money supply would contribute to unity and coherence, for money was "the vital principle of the body politic . . . which sustains its life and motion and enables it to perform its most essential functions." Central responsibility for commerce would ensure that "the veins of commerce in every part will be replenished and will acquire additional motion and vigour from a free circulation of the commodities of every part." Central management of the public debt would eliminate a "cause of collision" among the states. Such recent events as the Shays rebellion demonstrated that the nation must pull together lest it be pulled apart. "A NATION without a NATIONAL GOVERNMENT is, in my view, an awful spectacle."

The debate over ratification revealed the rifts in American politics more clearly than anything to date. A large part of the populace, while not happy at recent trends, feared more from a strong central government than from a weak one. A strong government, after all, was what the patriots of 1776 had rebelled against. What reasons could the ratification party give that Americans would be less tempted to abuse the powers of a strong government than the British had been? In this regard, Hamilton's pro-British reputation worked against him and his cause. The proceedings of the Philadelphia convention were supposed to have been secret, but reports leaked out of his praise for the British monarchy, which the rumor mills transformed into a desire to restore King George to an American throne. And when Hamilton insisted that the central government control money and taxes, veterans of the Revolution reminded the public that money and taxes were what the Revolution had been all about.

The Antifederalists, as Hamilton's opponents called themselves, mounted a furious fight. Many were open partisans of the democracy Hamilton derided, and they accused him and the Federalists of frustrating the will of the people. "The vast continent of America cannot long be subjected to a democracy if consolidated into one government," a New England Antifederalist asserted. "You might as well attempt to rule Hell by prayer." A Pennsylvania Antifederalist, distrustful of anything that enhanced government power, asserted, "The natural course of power is to make the many the slaves to the few." A South Carolinian asked an audience, "What have you been contending for these ten years? Liberty! What is liberty? The power of governing yourselves! If you adopt this constitution, have you the power?" The crowd roared, "No!!" Another Carolina audience expressed a similar view. "The people had a coffin painted black, which, borne in funeral procession, was solemnly buried as an emblem of the dissolution of public liberty," an eyewitness explained. "They feel that they are the very men who, as mere militia, half-armed and half-clothed, have fought and defeated the British regulars. . . . They think that after having disputed and gained the laurel under the banners of liberty, now they are likely to be robbed both of the honour and the fruits of it."

YET HAMILTON'S SIDE won, after some adroit political maneu-

vering (including a promise of a Bill of Rights), and the
Constitution was ratified. Hamilton thereupon urged a reluctant
George Washington, who wanted nothing more than to retire to
Mount Vernon, to heed the popular demand that he be president. Hamilton appealed to Washington's sense of duty and to
his vanity. If the new government failed after Washington stood
apart, he and the other Founders would incur "the disrepute of
having brought about a revolution in government without substi-
tuting anything that was worthy of the effort."

Washington consented, and won unanimous election (by the
electors, who in those days were chosen by the state legislatures
rather than the people). He promptly nominated Hamilton for
Treasury secretary. Hamilton was confirmed at once by the
Senate, and a week later the House of Representatives, the
chamber accorded primacy in money matters by the new
Constitution, asked him to submit a plan for reorganizing public
credit. The legislature then adjourned till January 1790, allowing Hamilton three months to organize his thoughts and prepare
his strategy.

When the lawmakers returned, Hamilton gave them more
than they had asked for. His "Report on Public Credit" proposed
a sweeping overhaul of American public finance, wrapped in an
audacious assertion of the centrality of capital to any stable government. Hamilton commenced by assaulting a notion dear to
democrats: that a public debt was a curse upon the body politic.
Far from it, he said. A public debt, properly funded, was a
"national blessing." In the first place, every country faced financial emergencies on occasion, when demands on the government

exceeded its revenues. Americans knew this better than most
people, having won their independence by means of a costly war.
Because the United States had lacked a credit history, and
because its government was so poorly organized, the interest it
had been required to pay on the money it borrowed had been
very high. Extrapolating from the wartime experience, Hamilton
explained, "When the credit of a country is in any degree ques-
tionable, it never fails to give an extravagant premium, in one
shape or another, upon all the loans it has occasion to make. Nor
does the evil end here; the same disadvantage must be sustained
on whatever is to be bought on terms of future payment."
American merchants had long known the value of a good credit
rating; Hamilton applied this basic commercial principle to the
national government.

Yet there was more to the value of public debt than lower
interest and prices. Government bonds made investors of those
who bought them, and investors naturally looked out for their
investments. These were precisely the sort who ought to be looking out for the federal government. "Those who are most commonly creditors of a nation are, generally speaking, enlightened
men," Hamilton asserted. By tying the material interest of such
enlightened men to the government, Hamilton aimed to guarantee the government's future. In this regard, it was essential that
the *federal* government borrow money, in order that all the bondholders pull in the same direction. "If all the public creditors
receive their dues from one source, distributed with an equal
hand, their interest will be the same," he said. "If, on the contrary, there are distinct provisions"—by the separate states—

"there will be distinct interests, drawing different ways. That union and concert of views, among the creditors, which in every Government is of great importance to their security, and that of public credit, will not only not exist, but will be likely to give place to mutual jealousy and opposition."

A public debt would serve yet another beneficent purpose. Though the Constitution explicitly granted the federal government the exclusive right to coin money, it said nothing about *printing* money. Because the United States lacked gold and silver mines, its economy depended for specie on trade with other countries. Hamilton advocated measures to expand trade (especially with Britain), but he recognized that under the best of circumstances, the supply of specie would never fulfill the requirements of America's rapidly growing economy. Paper was necessary. The war had demonstrated the dangers of fiat money, limited only by the stamina of the government's printers. Peace had alleviated but hadn't eradicated the problem, which was that officials answerable to the people preferred the course of least resistance in paying the people's bills. It was too much to ask of human nature to expect politicians to raise taxes when they could simply print more money.

A public debt would remove the temptation. Properly funded, the government notes would circulate essentially as money. Once the public became convinced that the notes would be redeemed at face value, any speculative discount would vanish. Moreover, the size of the debt—which was to say, the size of the money supply—would be under the control of the Treasury. In Hamilton's day, monetary theory was crude and inchoate, but

most of those who thought about the subject believed that a
money supply that grew at about the same speed as the productive capacity of the country yielded optimal economic perform-
ance. Until Hamilton, however, no one in America had proposed
a plausible scheme for managing the money supply.

Hamilton summarized the benefits his plan for managing
money would bring to the various activities and elements of
American society.

> Trade is extended by it, because there is a larger capital to
> carry it on, and the merchant can at the same time afford to
> trade for smaller profits. . . . Agriculture and manufactures are
> also promoted by it, for the like reason. . . . The interest of
> money will be lowered by it, for this is always in a ratio to the
> quantity of money and to the quickness of circulation. This
> circumstance will enable both the public and individuals to
> borrow on easier and cheaper terms. And from the combina-
> tion of these effects, additional aids will be furnished to
> labour, to industry, and to arts of every kind.

Hamilton's arguments mystified many of those lawmakers
who had spent less time than he contemplating the intricacies of
money. But none had difficulty comprehending the practical
measures he advocated for giving his theory effect. By Hamilton's
reckoning the public debt in 1790 stood at $79 million. More
than two-thirds of this—$54 million—was national debt; the rest
was owed by the states. Some of the debt was still held by its
original purchasers, many of whom had been motivated at least

in part by patriotism. But much had been purchased from the original owners by speculators at a steep discount. Hamilton proposed to redeem the debt at par—thereby delivering a windfall to the speculators. Moreover, he proposed to have the federal government take responsibility for the state notes, rolling the entire debt into a single package.

debt = fed's problem

He knew his plan wouldn't please everyone. "The case of those who parted with their securities from necessity, is a hard one," he granted. But what was the alternative to honoring the notes at full value? If the government paid the speculators only what *they* had paid, their risk in having purchased the notes would go unrewarded. If the government paid something to those who had sold the notes, the sellers would receive a bounty they had no right to expect. This course, moreover, entailed insuperable problems of locating original owners, determining the prices at which they had sold their notes, and distinguishing the ones who had sold on account of genuine necessity from those who had sold more opportunistically. Hamilton had no faith in the ability of government to make such distinctions. The market was a better mechanism. But the clinching argument against partial payment, in Hamilton's mind, was that it was actually partial default, which would gravely damage the credit of the new government and defeat a basic purpose of his plan.

argument

Hamilton's case for assuming the state debts followed from his belief that where investors' money lay, so lay their hearts. He didn't want the federal government competing with the states for capital, which would raise the cost of borrowing and divide the loyalties of the wealthy. Besides, the bulk of the state debts had been incurred in the national cause of independence; it therefore behooved the nation to pay them back. In addition, by barring the states from levying tariffs, the Constitution deprived them of their principal tool for funding repayment. Justice dictated that the federal government compensate them for their loss.

Hamilton appended a schedule of federal tariffs and excises as a way of supporting his debt program. He urged Congress to approve the schedule and the overall package. Time was of the essence, he said. Already European investors were snatching up American bonds and with them a claim on American resources. Should Congress procrastinate, "millions would probably be lost to the United States." But slow or late, provision for funding the public debt must come. The debt was the "price of liberty" and must be paid.

HAMILTON'S CREDIT PLAN split Congress and the country. Critics charged the Treasury secretary with wanting to deliver the republic into the hands of speculators, who even now were buying bonds by the basketful from straitened patriots who hadn't heard that Hamilton wanted to redeem them at par. "My soul arises indignant at the avaricious and immoral turpitude which so vile a conduct displays," James Jackson of Georgia told his colleagues in the House of Representatives. Congressman Benjamin Rush of Pennsylvania rejected Hamilton's praise of public credit. "It is to nations what private credit and loan offices are to individuals," Rush said. "It begets debt, extravagance, vice, and bankruptcy. . . . I sicken every time I contemplate the European vices that the

Secretary's gambling report will necessarily introduce into our
infant republic." William Maclay thought Hamilton's program
smacked of British arrogance. "He recommends indiscriminate
funding and in the style of a British minister has sent down his
bill," the Pennsylvania senator said. Maclay was convinced members of Congress were betting heavily on the bonds. "Henceforth
we may consider speculation as a congressional employment."
Maclay predicted that Hamilton would rue the day he drafted his
program. The "villainous business" of the public credit, Maclay
said, would "damn the character of Hamilton as a minister forever."

But it was the opposition of James Madison that mattered
most. Before and during the Constitutional Convention,
Madison had shared Hamilton's belief in the need for a stronger
national government, but now that he represented Virginia in the
House of Representatives he was reconsidering. Madison disliked
both of the central tenets of Hamilton's debt plan: the redemption
at par, with no distinction between original and subsequent purchasers, and the federal assumption of state debts. The former
insulted civic virtue, Madison contended, by penalizing patriots
and rewarding speculators. The patriots, those original purchasers, would be doubly damaged: by their opportunity loss at
having relinquished the notes, and by their share of the taxes
required to pay the speculators. The assumption plan similarly
harmed the virtuous, in that some states—including Madison's
Virginia—had honestly striven to pay off their debts, while others
had profligately let the debts slide. Hamilton's assumption
scheme would make the thrifty states pay twice: once for the
debts they had already redeemed, twice in the taxes to pay other

states' debts. Madison wrote his objections into amendments to Hamilton's funding plan. One amendment discriminated between original purchasers and speculators; the other blocked assumption and left the states to pay their own debts.

Madison's discrimination amendment struck many of his House colleagues as morally worthy but practically unworkable, and it was quickly voted down. His anti-assumption amendment fared better. The Antifederalist suspicion of an encroaching federal government had definitely not disappeared upon ratification of the Constitution, and the very arguments Hamilton employed in favor of assumption—particularly that it would attach investors to the central government rather than to the states—seemed to the skeptics good reason to reject it. An emerging sectionalism also supported Madison against assumption. The southern states, dominated by planters with their feet firmly in the soil, considered themselves more fiscally responsible than their northern neighbors, where capitalists frolicked in the bustling cities. This perception wasn't entirely accurate; many planters were over their heads in debt, and South Carolina contained a cadre of capitalists who backed Hamilton. But the perception influenced enough votes in the House to allow Madison to defeat the assumption part of Hamilton's plan in a preliminary ballot.

Hamilton took the setback personally. He felt betrayed by Madison and began muttering against him as a "clever man" but "very little acquainted with the world." The debt plan, Hamilton believed, was indivisible. "Credit is an *entire thing*," he said. "Every part of it has the nicest sympathy with every other part. Wound one limb and the whole tree shrinks and decays."

Yet rather than concede Madison the victory, Hamilton
enlisted the support of Thomas Jefferson, Washington's secretary
of state. Before long a deep rift would divide Hamilton from
Jefferson, but in the summer of 1790 they were merely cautious
of each other. Washington encouraged camaraderie, at least
occasionally. In June he took the Cabinet fishing on the Hudson
(the federal government was based in New York at that time) in
order that the bass and blackfish make good sports, if not necessarily good sportsmen, of his secretaries.

Something must have worked, for Jefferson determined to
intercede with Madison on Hamilton's behalf. Hamilton had
grown discouraged over the prospects of assumption, and when
Jefferson encountered him on Broadway near the house
Washington had rented, he seemed worn and worried. He told
Jefferson that the New England states were threatening to bolt
the Union if assumption weren't approved. As for himself, he
thought he'd have to resign if his credit plan failed to pass intact.
He said that Jefferson had as much stake as he did in the success
of the administration, and he hoped he could count on the secretary of state's cooperation. Jefferson was hardly happier about
assumption than Madison was, but as a member of the administration rather than a member of the House, he felt less beholden
to those Virginians who despised Hamilton's scheme. He agreed
to do what he could.

A short while later he invited Hamilton and Madison to join
him for dinner. Precisely what was said there has puzzled histo-
rians since. But two issues that had been vexing Congress—
assumption and the location of the national capital—were

resolved not long after dessert. The Virginians wanted the capital in their part of the country lest the capitalists of New York and Philadelphia carry the government away. Those capitalists demanded assumption. The bargain apparently struck at Jefferson's table gave the northerners assumption and the southerners the capital. For ten years the government would meet at Philadelphia, but in 1800 it would move to the Potomac.

None of the three admitted at the time that a deal had been made. Madison continued to vote against assumption. Hamilton treated the location of the capital as an entirely separate matter. Jefferson kept his role in bringing the two men together a secret. Only later, after the decisive votes on both issues shifted columns and the measures passed, did the matter come to light. "This is the real history of the assumption," Jefferson acknowledged.

A LESS AMBITIOUS man might have counted his good fortune and left Congress and the American political system to digest its financial meal. Yet Hamilton impatiently pushed forward. Federal debt might circulate *almost* as money, but it wasn't the real thing. The Treasury could manage the debt, but Congress determined its overall size. This left entirely too much discretion in the hands of the democrats, in Hamilton's view. To diminish the democratic influence, he proposed a national bank.

Hamilton had been studying up on public banks, especially in the writings of Adam Smith. In the landmark treatise *The Wealth of Nations,* the Scottish godfather of modern capitalism wrote

BANK OF THE U.S.

that the Bank of England acted "not only as an ordinary bank, but
as a great engine of state," handling government tax accounts,
paying interest on the government's debt, and circulating bank
notes that served as currency. Hamilton thought a Bank of the
United States could do the same. "Such a Bank," he wrote in a
message delivered to Congress in December 1790, "is not a mere
matter of private property, but a political machine of the greatest
importance to the State." Hamilton's bank would receive taxes,
disburse appropriations, manage the national debt, and issue
notes that would serve as money.

This last function was the critical one, and the one that most
required explaining. Banks were relatively new to America. The
first, the Bank of Pennsylvania, hadn't been founded till 1780,
and at the time of Hamilton's writing, only three banks existed.
Banks were mysterious institutions that swallowed specie and
regurgitated paper. This by itself made them objects of popular
suspicion. The fact that bankers got rich in the process, without
doing anything that looked like work to the large majority of
Americans who bent and sweated for their living, made the
banks seem more suspicious still. If Hamilton hoped to get his
bank, he needed to educate the members of Congress on the
good that banks could do not only for themselves and their owners but for society as a whole.

He dove right in. He described the functions of banks in
detail, starting with the most important and least understood:
"the augmentation of the active or productive capital of a country." As useful as gold and silver were when circulated as money,
they were essentially dead—unable to multiply—compared to

what they became when deposited or invested in a bank. "They then acquire life, or, in other words, an active and productive quality," Hamilton said.

> The money which the merchant keeps in his chest, waiting for a favorable opportunity to employ it, produces nothing till that opportunity arrives. But if, instead of locking it up in this manner, he either deposits it in a bank, or invests it in the stock of a bank, it yields a profit. . . . His money, thus deposited or invested, is a fund upon which himself and others can borrow to a much larger amount.

Any bank might perform this function, but a national bank could perform it particularly well. The notes of a national bank could circulate throughout the country more readily than those of a bank chartered in a single state. In addition, a national bank would manage the accounts of the federal government, giving it access to greater reserves, and therefore enabling it to sustain a larger supply of paper notes, than other banks.

From the standpoint of the federal government, a national bank allowed a fine-tuning of the money supply impossible to achieve by other means. Hamilton reiterated his belief that politicians answerable to the people couldn't be trusted with the power to print money. Yet he had to be careful not to insult the legislators, and so he spoke of an extreme case, a "great and trying emergency" calling for extraordinary expenditures. "The stamping of paper is an operation so much easier than the laying of taxes, that a Government, in the practice of paper emissions, would rarely fail, in any such emergency, to indulge itself too far in the employment of that resource, to avoid, as much as possible, one less auspicious to present popularity." The beauty of a bank was that its paper issues were—or would be, under Hamilton's scheme—tied to its supply of specie. Only by increasing its reserves could the bank expand the money it circulated. Hamilton acknowledged that nothing in the Constitution forbade Congress from issuing fiat money. But the states were prohibited from doing so, "and the spirit of that prohibition ought not to be disregarded by the Government of the United States."

Hamilton realized that banks labored under a burden of popular distrust, which he attempted to diminish. Did banks increase usury, as was often charged? Sometimes they did, he conceded. But this was a consequence of their newness in

Alexander Hamilton at the height of his self-esteem. The document under his right hand is perhaps his proposal for the Bank of the United States.

America. "Experience and practice generally bring a cure to this evil." Indeed, Hamilton's plan, by expanding the money supply in a measured way, would reduce interest rates as lenders no longer felt obliged to include an inflation premium. Did banks encourage speculation? Sometimes, but here again a more stable money supply would remedy most of the problem. Did banks cause gold and silver to disappear from circulation? Hamilton didn't deny it. But this was a good thing, at least in the case of well-run banks, for the specie hidden in the bank vaults supported a much larger paper currency and therefore much greater economic activity. In any case, he said, wise legislators ought not to become obsessed with what might go wrong. "If the abuses of a beneficial thing are to determine its condemnation, there is scarcely a source of public prosperity which will not be speedily closed."

As he had with his debt plan, Hamilton included details in his bank proposal. The bank would be capitalized at $10 million, divided into 25,000 shares worth $400 each. These would be sold by subscription to individuals and to groups. The president of the United States would be authorized to purchase on behalf of the American public $2 million of the bank's stock, or one-fifth. Twenty-five percent of the price of any purchase must be in gold or silver; the rest could be in federal securities. The bank would have twenty-five directors, elected by the stockholders according to the number of shares they held. Hamilton couldn't require the public to accept the paper issued by the bank, but he attempted the next best thing by proposing that "the bills and notes of the Bank . . . shall be receivable in all payments to the United States."

IN THE SEVERAL months since the fight over Hamilton's debt plan, the opposition to his pro-business policies had firmed up. Much of the agrarian South now deemed his bank a plot by the capitalist North to make the federal government its plaything. The echoes of the colonial past were ominous. "What was it drove our forefathers to this country?" asked Georgia's James Jackson. "Was it not the ecclesiastical corporations and perpetual monopolies of England and Scotland? Shall we suffer the same evils to exist in this country?" Approving Hamilton's bank would do no less. Hamilton had contended that his bank would serve the general welfare. "What is the general welfare?" Jackson demanded. "It is the welfare of Philadelphia, New York, and Boston." As for the other regions: "They may as well be out of the Union, as to any advantages they will receive from the institution."

James Madison took a different tack, portraying the bank as unconstitutional. Madison reminded the House that the Tenth Amendment—which he had drafted, along with the rest of the Bill of Rights—declared that those powers not delegated to the federal government by the Constitution were reserved "to the states respectively or the people." Madison scrutinized his copy of the Constitution and found nothing pertaining to bank charters (or corporate charters of any sort). He concluded that Hamilton's scheme "was condemned by the silence of the Constitution, was condemned by the rule of interpretation arising out of the Constitution, was condemned by its tendency to destroy the main characteristic of the Constitution." Madison hoped "it would receive its final condemnation by the vote of this House."

George Washington asked Jefferson whether he agreed that Hamilton's bank was unconstitutional. The secretary of state said he did. He conceded that a national bank might facilitate the operations of government, but this hardly decided the matter. "A little difference in the degree of convenience cannot constitute the necessity which the Constitution makes the ground for assuming any non-enumerated power," Jefferson said. "Nothing but a necessity invincible by any other means can justify such a prostration of laws which constitute the pillars of our whole system of jurisprudence."

Hamilton listened and read with silent glee. The opponents of the bank, by resting their case on the Constitution rather than on the merits of the bank, had given him the opportunity to play to Washington's prejudices and kill a flock of birds with a single stone. As a Virginia planter, Washington sympathized with the opponents of the bank as a bank; but as president of the United States, he had an interest in a broad interpretation of the Constitution. Hamilton gave him just that.

This *general principle* is *inherent* in the very *definition* of *Government* and *essential* to every step of the progress to be made by that of the United States, namely that every power vested in a Government is in its nature *sovereign,* and includes by *force* of the *term,* a right to employ all the *means* requisite and fairly *applicable* to the attainment of the *ends* of such power, and which are not precluded by restrictions and exceptions specified in the constitution, or not immoral, or not contrary to the essential ends of society.

In other words, what the Constitution didn't explicitly deny was implicitly allowed to those in power.

With this statement Hamilton drew the line that would forever separate strict constructionists from loose constructionists—those who sought to curb the power of the national government from those who wished to expand it. Strikingly, in Hamilton's day the capitalists stood on the loose side of the line, aiming to extend the powers of government in support of their financial and mercantile activities. The democrats arrayed themselves opposite, trying to contain government and limit its powers.

Whether the endorsement of Hamilton's bank bill was a victory for loose construction was less clear. It passed both the Senate and the House with relative ease, but partly because many legislators saw it as a way to make a personal profit. Thirty members of Congress—more than a third of the total membership, and half of those who voted in favor—became charter shareholders. This hardly surprised the strict-construction opponents of the bank. Power corrupted, they said, and no power corrupted more quickly than the money power. After Washington, persuaded by Hamilton, signed the bank bill into law, they held their breath for the fate of the republic.

2

The Bank War

T he fight over the Bank of the United States marked the beginning of the end of the fondest dream of the Founders: that the country they created might be spared the rancor of partisan politics. Parties, they believed, were artifacts of monarchy, where competing interests vied for the king's favor. In a republic, based on civic virtue, parties need never emerge, for all good citizens would seek the common weal. What the Founders failed to appreciate was that good citizens might have distinctly different visions of the common weal. In time Americans would accept this conclusion, but enough of the Revolutionary idealism remained during the 1790s to cause opposing camps of idealists to condemn their opponents as base, malicious, and corrupt.

Heading the camp of capitalism was Hamilton; of democracy, Jefferson. Hamilton's Federalists favored a strong central government attuned to commerce and finance; their geographic base was New England and the cities. Jefferson's party, which called itself the Republicans, strove to limit federal power and tilted toward farmers, including the planters of the South, where the Republican center of gravity lay. The fault line between the parties assumed an international angle when the French Revolution led to war in Europe. The Federalists followed Hamilton in perceiving a natural affinity between the moneyed classes of America and those of Britain; from this perception flowed a preference for Britain in this latest installment of that country's historic struggle with France. The Republicans favored France, on grounds of gratitude for French help in the American Revolutionary War, of continuing hostility toward past master Britain, and especially of revolutionary France's endorsement of the principles of popular government on which the American republic had been founded. When the British and the French both began preying on American shipping, with each trying to deny American trade to the other, the foreign-policy debate became passionately vitriolic. The Federalists alleged Republican complicity in the French Reign of Terror; the Republicans imagined Federalist plots to reattach America to the British empire.

The fierceness of partisan politics in America dismayed the oldest Founders. George Washington shook his head and retired to Mount Vernon. "Me thought I heard him think, 'Ay! I am fairly out and you are fairly in!'" John Adams recorded upon succeeding Washington in the presidency. "'See which of us will be the happiest!'" Adams soon envied Washington. After he and the Federalist majority in Congress took the French seizures of American ships as cause to launch an undeclared naval war against France, the Republicans cried sellout to Britain. The Federalists responded by ramming through Congress the Alien and Sedition Acts, outlawing most dissent. Jefferson, Adams's vice president—under the original system for choosing presidents, whereby the runner-up became vice president—secretly penned a protest asserting the right of states to nullify laws they deemed unconstitutional. Jefferson then challenged Adams's reelection, initiating one of the nastiest campaigns in American political history.

Hamilton took part in the campaign but not, surprisingly, on Adams's side. After his twin triumphs on the debt and the Bank of the United States, Hamilton's star had fallen somewhat. A proposal by him for the encouragement of manufacturing in America, by federal subsidies to capitalists and protective tariffs against imports, struck even some of his Federalist friends as excessive and fell dead in Congress. An adulterous affair led to blackmail by the husband of Hamilton's paramour, quietly curbing Hamilton's ambitions; when the affair and the blackmail payments surfaced, his enemies were delighted and his supporters embarrassed. During the hostilities with France, Adams recalled Washington to service as commander of the army; Washington consented on condition that Hamilton be his inspector general. In this post Hamilton proposed to employ the troops against those who challenged federal authority on the Alien and Sedition Acts. The mere idea outraged the Republicans and unnerved more than a few of the Federalists; when Washington resigned the army command, Adams conspicuously snubbed Hamilton by leaving the position vacant. Hamilton struck back during the campaign of 1800, circulating a pamphlet slashing Adams unmercifully. "There are great and intrinsic defects in his character which make him unfit for the office of Chief Magistrate," Hamilton wrote. "By his ill humours and jealousies he has already divided and distracted the supporters of the Government. . . . He has furnished deadly weapons to its enemies by unfounded accusations, and has weakened the force of its friends by decrying some of the most influential of them to the utmost of his power."

Hamilton's pamphlet guaranteed Adams's defeat. Jefferson triumphed over Adams in the 1800 balloting, but to the confusion of the Republicans, the pleasure of the Federalists, and the puzzlement of most Americans, Jefferson finished in an electoral tie with Aaron Burr. The Constitution specified that each elector should have two votes. Jefferson was the clear favorite of the Republican electors, who also favored New Yorker Burr for vice president. One of the electors was supposed to toss away his second vote, to ensure that Jefferson finish first and Burr second. But communications snarled, and Burr received as many votes as Jefferson. This threw the contest to the House of Representatives, where lame-duck and now mischief-bent Federalists still ruled. Only the intervention of Hamilton, who considered Jefferson foolish but Burr dangerous, broke the deadlock, in Jefferson's favor.

Hamilton subsequently learned just how dangerous Burr was. Burr nursed his injury for three years, during which he fell out with Jefferson, who grew almost as alarmed at Burr's ambition as Hamilton already was. Aware he wouldn't receive a second term for vice president, Burr ran for governor of New York. Hamilton continued to oppose him, in language that cast aspersions on Burr's character. Burr lost and thereupon challenged Hamilton to a duel. Hamilton's eldest son had died in a duel, and Hamilton agonized at possibly subjecting his wife to another such tragedy. But his honor wouldn't let him refuse. On the morning of July 11, 1804, Burr and Hamilton met at Weehawken, New Jersey (dueling being illegal in New York). Burr's bullet ruptured Hamilton's liver and lodged in his spine. He lingered in pain before dying the next day.

THE DUEL ENDED Burr's political career almost as quickly as it ended Hamilton's life. A New York grand jury indicted him, and he fled for his freedom to the West. He stopped in Philadelphia, where he took refuge in the home of Charles Biddle, a descendant of Quakers and an old friend. By happenstance the Biddle household at just that moment included Nicholas Biddle, Charles Biddle's eighteen-year-old-son, who had been living away at college and was about to sail for France. Young Nick was seeking a path in life and had been contemplating politics. But the extremist turn of party affairs, embodied in the Biddle house by the bloodstained vice president, prompted a somber reconsideration. "The violence of party . . . disgraces our country," he wrote. He wanted nothing to do with it.

He proceeded to Paris, to become the personal secretary of the American minister to France. The United States had recently arranged to purchase Louisiana from France, and Nick was assigned to help sort out the financial details. He dealt with merchants, particularly those who had claims subsumed in the $15 million purchase price, and bankers, including representatives of Barings, the London house that underwrote the transaction. Eventually he worked himself out of a job and, after a grand tour of the Continent, returned to Philadelphia.

He again felt the urge to public service. "Every good citizen owes himself to his country," he wrote. But he still shuddered at the violence of party politics, and so he chose the world of literature instead. The *Port Folio,* a genteel journal of arts and lofty criticism, offered him its editorship. He accepted. Between issues he studied law.

Yet public service wouldn't let him escape so easily, and after friends and professional associates pleaded with him to accept nomination to the lower house of the Pennsylvania legislature, he entered politics. He was elected in time to observe the demise of one of Philadelphia's landmark institutions. The national capital had moved on schedule in 1800 to Washington City (as it was called while the memory of Washington the man lingered), but the Bank of the United States remained in Philadelphia. Its stranding was more than physical, for the Republicans who had controlled the federal government since Jefferson's election made clear they wouldn't renew the Bank's charter when it expired in 1811.

Biddle's politics and economics were Hamiltonian (notwithstanding his father's kindness to Hamilton's killer), and as a Pennsylvania lawmaker he lamented the decision to let the Bank die. A recent exacerbation of the troubles between the United

States and Britain had led some Americans to call for war; Biddle
didn't agree, but he thought the possibility of war made dissolution of the Bank especially inopportune. "Is this a time to disorder the finances?" he inquired rhetorically. "When the nerves of
the whole nation should be braced and strong, are we to prepare
for combat by cutting the main artery of all its resources?"

James Madison, who had succeeded Jefferson as president,
and the other Republicans ignored Biddle, and the Bank concluded its operations. Yet hardly had the doors been bolted and
the windows shuttered than the administration began having
second thoughts. The war clouds burst in 1812, and the ensuing
conflict severely strained the finances of the federal government.
At first the government benefited from Hamilton's earlier efforts
on behalf of the public credit, but as the fighting persisted
Madison succumbed to the temptation Hamilton had warned of
and began printing unsupported paper money. Interest rates
soared, investor confidence plunged, and the national accounts
spun into confusion. That the war went badly for American military forces compounded the financial chaos, and about the time
the British burned the Capitol and the White House, Madison
concluded that Hamilton had been right regarding the need for
a national bank, at least in time of crisis. Conveniently forgotten
were the earlier Republican assertions, most notably by Madison
himself, that a national bank contravened the Constitution.

Ironically, however, Hamilton's heirs in the Federalist party
now opposed a national bank. Some complained that the
Republicans, ignorant of the first principles of banking, failed to
afford the institution adequate funds. "This Bank is to begin with

insolvency," Daniel Webster declared. "It is to commence its existence in dishonor. It is to draw its first breath in disgrace." At least as much of the opposition, though, reflected the growth of state banks since the closing of the first Bank of the United States, and the Federalists' political and often financial attachment to those local institutions.

But the opposition failed, and in 1816 the second Bank of the United States was chartered. Its terms were similar to those of the first, but not identical. The Bank's capital was $35 million, rather than $10 million, reflecting the growth in the nation's economy since 1791. The federal government would still own twenty percent of the stock, and the Bank would still have twenty-five directors. But only twenty of the directors would be elected; the other five would be appointed by the president.

ONE OF THOSE appointed directors, starting in 1819, was Nicholas Biddle. He took the job reluctantly. He had never lost his distaste for the roughhouse of politics, and the first two years of operation had made the new Bank the target of heated criticism. State banks claimed that the national bank stole their business. Debtors denounced the Bank's efforts to strengthen the currency. When convincing evidence emerged that some of the directors of the Bank had engaged in speculation in the Bank's stock and even outright fraud, Republican skeptics of banks and bankers recycled their complaints from Hamilton's day that the national bank was a plot against the American people.

Biddle appreciated the need to fix the Bank. "That it has been perverted to selfish purposes cannot be doubted," he wrote President James Monroe upon learning that Monroe wanted to nominate him for director. "That it may, and must, be renovated is equally certain." But the renovations wouldn't come easily. "They who undertake to reform abuses . . . must encounter much hostility." Biddle wasn't sure he could handle the criticism. Yet when Monroe appealed to his patriotism, Biddle decided he couldn't resist. "I am unwilling to avoid any duty by which you think I can be of service," he told the president.

The timing of Biddle's appointment could hardly have been less auspicious. In 1819 the United States suffered its first full-blown financial panic. The American economy had grown by fits and starts since the end of the Revolutionary War, with farming continuing to employ the great majority of Americans, commerce supporting a smaller but substantial number, and various kinds of manufacturing beginning to play a role. The farm economy expanded by virtue of the rapid increase of both the population and the land area of the United States. The former had roughly doubled since the Revolution, as a result of natural increase and immigration; the latter had doubled, too, upon the acquisition of Louisiana from France. Commerce increased apace, although the chronic wars between Britain and France put a crimp on overseas trade. Manufacturing emerged with the introduction of new technology—the cotton gin, for example, and mechanical looms—and the disappearance, upon American independence, of the restrictions Britain had placed on colonial manufactures.

The War of 1812 put a damper on the economic growth. Commodities clogged American warehouses as exporters refused to run the British blockade. The inflation induced by the war—or, rather, by the Madison administration's wartime monetary policies—dislocated nearly every sector of the economy, deranging prices and making rational business planning impossible.

The derangement took a new form after the war. Though the conflict against Britain ended in a standoff, the accompanying struggle against the Indians of the West culminated in the destruction of nearly all aboriginal resistance to white settlement east of the Mississippi. The sudden availability of vast new reaches of territory, combined with the loose money left over from the war, fueled wild speculation in land. Prices rose and rose, becoming unsustainable about the time Biddle joined the board of the second Bank of the United States. Nervous lenders, including the Bank, insisted on stronger collateral; this reminder of reality ruined the fun and threw the speculation into reverse. Land prices plummeted, causing everything erected upon them to collapse as well. Banks called in their loans and savers hoarded, driving prices still further down. Solid figures on the overall shrinkage of the money supply are impossible to reconstruct, but the contraction of the liabilities of the Bank of the United States—from $22 million in the autumn of 1818 to $10 million at the beginning of 1820—is indicative.

The depression that followed the panic prostrated large parts of the country. Banks folded; merchants liquidated; sailing ships sat idle; commercial buildings stood empty; farmers lost their land and homes. Tens of thousands of Americans took to the roads in vague hope of finding something better than the disaster they fled. An Ohioan described "distress . . . beyond comprehension. Marshal and sheriff sales are almost daily." An observer in western New York lamented the sight of "families naked . . . children freezing in the winter's storm . . . fathers without coats or shoes."

The one bright spot of the season, for the Bank of the United States if not for the destitute, was a decision by the Supreme Court regarding the Bank's constitutionality. The change of Republican heart in Washington that had allowed the resurrection of the Bank didn't extend to all the states, several of which passed laws to inhibit its operation. Maryland taxed banks not chartered by Maryland's legislature, of which the Bank of the United States was the prime example. James McCulloch, the cashier of the Baltimore branch of the Bank, refused to pay the tax. Maryland sued, McCulloch countersued, and the case went to the Supreme Court.

Chief Justice John Marshall had been appointed by John Adams just before that last Federalist president left office in 1801. For nearly two decades Marshall had defended and elaborated the Federalist vision of a strong central government. As his Federalist colleagues on the Supreme Court retired and died, he grew lonelier but more adamant that the nation took precedence over the states and that the Constitution allowed what it didn't explicitly forbid. This was the line he adopted in leading the court to rule for McCulloch and the Bank. "Let the end be legitimate," Marshall wrote (in words that echoed Hamilton's justification of the first Bank), "let it be within the scope of the Constitution, and all means which are appropriate, which are plainly adapted to that end, which are not prohibited, but consist

with the letter and spirit of the Constitution, are constitutional."
The Bank fit Marshall's description and therefore was constitutional. As for the Maryland law taxing the Bank, it was not. "The
power to tax involves the power to destroy," Marshall wrote. If a
state could tax the operations of the federal government, it could
prevent those operations. "This was not intended by the
American people. They did not intend to make their government
dependent on the states."

A more forthright declaration of the Hamiltonian view, not
only on the Bank but on the powers of the federal government
at large, was difficult to imagine. Many Republicans disputed
Marshall's interpretation, and decades would pass before the
Supreme Court was generally accepted as the final arbiter of
the Constitution. But in the meantime Marshall's opinion gave the
Bank a continued lease on life.

NICHOLAS BIDDLE MADE the most of Marshall's ruling. In
1822 the Bank board required a new president, and Biddle, as a
voting member, reflected on the requisites for the job. Chief
among these, he decided, were "talent for business, standing
with the government, and residence in Philadelphia." The need
for business talent in the Bank president was obvious, although
Biddle noted that this wasn't confined to "men of business," who
seemed to him often to lack vision. As for the Bank president's
relation to government: "He should be known to and stand well
with the Government—not an active partisan, not even a party
man—but a man in whom the Government would confide. I am

far from thinking that the government should have any direct or indirect influence over the Bank. On the contrary, the less of it which exists, the better for both. But the government is a great stockholder and a great customer." Regarding Philadelphia residence: the Bank was headquartered there, and a Philadelphian would foster good relations with the community.

Having characterized the ideal Bank president, Biddle decided he fit the bill as well as anyone, and at the encouragement of some of the directors he let his name be put forward. In January 1823, two days before his thirty-seventh birthday, he became president of the Bank of the United States.

His promotion elicited skepticism in some moneyed quarters. John Jacob Astor, the New York merchant and real-estate developer who was on his way to becoming America's richest man, thought Biddle too literary to run the nation's leading bank. Biddle responded in good-humored verse, elevating living financiers over dead authors.

I prefer my last letters from Barings or Hope
To the finest epistles of Pliny or Pope.

Biddle added that he had abandoned illusions of art's transcendence and found peace and happiness in "that simplest, sublimest of truths—six per cent."

As his first order of business, Biddle oversaw completion of the Bank's new headquarters, a marble-columned structure on Philadelphia's Chestnut Street. And amid a belated but general revival of business after the post-1819 depression, he directed the consolidation of the Bank's resources and the reestablishment of its role as the balance wheel of the American economy. One measure of his success was the reduction and eventual elimination of the monetary exchange rate between the different regions of the country. Eastern merchants and bankers had long discounted western bank notes, both because of the trouble involved in redeeming them and because western banks were perceived to be riskier than their eastern counterparts. Biddle's Bank, by transferring funds efficiently and by enforcing uniform standards among its various branches, brought the regions into alignment.

This accomplishment pleased many but alienated others. The brokers who had profited from the differential took offense, as did the friends of state banks whose business was stolen by Biddle's Bank. Unreconstructed Jeffersonians, distrusting all banks, interpreted this exercise of Biddle's power as a threat to democracy.

The hero of this last group was Andrew Jackson, who knew next to nothing about banks, a little more about money, and a great deal about democracy. By the 1820s nearly all the old property qualifications for voting had disappeared, as new states entered the Union with constitutions based on the egalitarian rhetoric of the Declaration of Independence, and shamed the existing states into changing their rules. At the same time and for similarly democratic reasons, state legislatures conferred the selection of presidential electors upon the people. The result was that presidential campaigns in the 1820s became popularity contests, with the victor the candidate most appealing to the largest number of adult white males.

Occasionally the system stumbled. Though Jackson garnered the most popular votes in 1824, he split the electoral vote with three other candidates, and the race went to the House of Representatives, from which John Quincy Adams emerged victorious. Adams wasn't as hostile to democracy as his Federalist father, John Adams, had been, but he was certainly less populist than Jackson. And when he appointed Henry Clay, the fourth-place finisher, who had thrown his support to Adams in the House, to be secretary of state and thereby—in the practice of those days—heir apparent to the presidency, the Jacksonians cried "corrupt bargain." They lashed the Adams-Clay cabal for perverting democracy and commenced the campaign of 1828 at once.

IN THAT CAMPAIGN Biddle supported Adams, but silently. "There is no one principle better understood by every officer in the Bank than that he must abstain from politics," Biddle told an associate.

> The course of the Bank is very clear and straight on that point. We believe that the prosperity of the Bank and its usefulness to the country depend on its being entirely free from the control of the officers of the Government, a control fatal to every bank which it ever influenced. In order to preserve that independence it must never connect itself with any administration, and never become a partisan of any set of politicians. . . . We have no concern in politics. Dean Swift said, you know,

that money is neither Whig nor Tory, and we say with equal
truth that the Bank is neither Jackson man nor Adams man. It
is only a bank.

Yet the Bank *wasn't* only a bank. It was the arbiter of the
nation's money supply, the bestower or withholder of prosperity.
Biddle wouldn't have had it otherwise.

But Andrew Jackson would. Jackson hadn't said much about
the Bank during the campaign; in fact he hadn't said much about
any issues. Jackson adopted the position pioneered by that other
general-turned-politician, George Washington, that a candidate's
actions and character should speak for themselves. Jackson recognized, moreover, that his value to voters as a symbol of the triumph of democracy would only diminish once he descended into
the realm of policy. As a result, when he assumed the presidency
in 1829 after an easy defeat of Adams, he did so unburdened by
promises or commitments to anything more specific than the
national welfare, however he chose to define it.

On the money question, the defining began with Jackson's first
annual message (the written equivalent of what would come to be
called the State of the Union address). The president reminded
the country that the charter of the Bank of the United States
would expire in 1836, and he supposed that the stockholders
would apply for a renewal of the charter. He warned them to
expect a presidential veto. A strict constructionist, Jackson
believed that Congress legitimately might charter a bank for the
federal District of Columbia, but not for the rest of the country.

That John Marshall had ruled otherwise didn't impress him.

Biddle read Jackson's remarks yet didn't take them seriously. "They should be treated as the honest though erroneous notions of one who intends well," Biddle told a friend. He assumed that when the sager heads in the administration and the president's party asserted themselves, they would side with the Bank. "The expressions in the message were the President's own, not dictated nor suggested by any body else, and asserted in opposition to the wishes, if not the advice, of all his habitual counselors. It is not therefore a cabinet measure, nor a party measure, but a personal measure. As such it is far less dangerous." Once people understood this, all would be well. "The question will be decided on its own merits."

Here Biddle was the naïve one. Few questions in American politics are decided on their merits alone, and the Bank question was not one of those. Henry Clay still wanted to be president, and he befriended the Bank to that end. Clay's embrace of what he called the "American system" of federal support for business via protective tariffs and funding for roads, bridges, and canals made him Kentucky's answer to Alexander Hamilton—only taller, handsomer, and more eloquent—and extended easily to the Bank. As the leader of the anti-Jackson party in Congress, Clay nominated himself as Biddle's chief legislative adviser. He told Biddle to move slowly on renewal of the charter. Though Biddle had the votes in Congress, Clay said, Jackson's warning of a veto had to be taken seriously. Presidential vetoes were rare in those early days but not unheard of; in fact Jackson had just vetoed a roads bill, on the ground that internal improvements were constitutionally reserved to the states. He might well veto Bank renewal. The question then would be "referred to the people," Clay said, "and would inevitably mix itself with all our elections. It would probably become . . . the controlling question in American politics. The friends of the Bank would have to argue the question before the public against the official act of the President, and against the weight of his popularity." The Bank couldn't win such a contest. Better to wait, therefore, till after the election of 1832. "Then everything will be fresh; the succeeding Presidential election will be too remote to be a shaping measure in reference to it; and there will be a disposition to afford the new administration the facilities in our fiscal affairs which the Bank of the United States perhaps alone can render." Clay was already running to replace Jackson; his assurance on the Bank was to let Biddle know that a President Clay would be cooperative. But even if Jackson were returned to office, the Bank would be better off for having waited. "He will have probably less disposition than he has now to avail himself of any prejudices against the Bank. He will then also have less influence, for it may be loosely asserted, at least as a general rule, that the President will have less popularity in his second than in his first term."

Clay may have been giving Biddle honest advice in this letter. Everything he said was plausible enough. But Clay was also pursuing his own self-interest. With the election two years away, he didn't want to have to run as the defender of the Bank and capital against Jackson as the champion of democracy and the people. Clay concurred with Biddle that the Bank served the national interest, but he didn't expect the masses to agree. And those masses were the ones who, for better or worse, now controlled America's destiny.

Perhaps surprisingly, Biddle had greater confidence in the masses than Clay did. After Jackson repeated his warning about terminating the Bank, Biddle wrote defiantly, "In respect to General Jackson and Mr. Van Buren"—Secretary of State Martin Van Buren, whom Jackson was grooming for the succession—"I have not the slightest fear of either of them. . . . Our countrymen are not naturally disposed to cut their own throats to please any body, and I have so perfect a reliance on the spirit and sense of the nation that I think we can defend the institution from much stronger enemies than they are." All that was necessary was education. "We must endeavour to reach the understandings of our fellow citizens by the diffusion of correct views of a subject which is much misunderstood."

Biddle didn't have quite the faith in his countrymen to conduct his educational campaign overtly. He utilized Bank funds to pay for the drafting of pro-Bank articles conveying, as he put it, "real and positive information regarding the working of the institution and its beneficial influence on the prosperity of the nation." He offered editors up to a thousand dollars to insert such articles in their papers. He asked only that his role in the campaign be concealed, "as it might be misconstrued."

Biddle's campaign also involved payments to politicians. Daniel Webster, who had represented the Bank in the McCulloch Supreme Court case, now represented Massachusetts in the Senate. Biddle placed him on the payroll—as Webster reminded him rather brusquely when an installment was delayed. "I believe my retainer has not been renewed, or *refreshed,* as usual," Webster wrote. "If it be wished that my relation to the Bank should be continued, it may be well to send me the usual retainers."

Finally, by way of a warning to the enemies of the Bank to keep hands off, Biddle arranged a contraction of credit in the West. It was there that antipathy for the Bank ran broadest and support for Jackson deepest. Biddle concealed his intentions in the matter, citing financial uncertainty as cause for calling in the loans. The effect wasn't dramatic but it was unmistakable, as was Biddle's point: that the Bank would defend itself, by harming its enemies if necessary.

AS THE ELECTION of 1832 approached, Jackson remained as popular as ever, to Henry Clay's discouragement. Clay had hoped for a slip, an opening for attack. But nothing significant developed, and he gradually realized that the only way to prevent Jackson's reelection was to start a political brushfire, in hopes Jackson would stumble trying to put it out. He reversed his earlier advice to Biddle about delaying renewal of the Bank's charter. Biddle could still anticipate cooperation in Congress, Clay said. As to Jackson: "My own belief is that, if *now* called upon, he would not negative the bill, but that if he should be re-elected the event might and probably would be different." Clay adduced no evidence in support of this belief. And in fact he had none. But he did have the recent nomination of the National Republicans—as the anti-Jacksonians currently styled

themselves—on a platform calling the Bank a "great and beneficent institution," and he hoped to make the Bank the central
issue in his campaign for president.

Biddle bit. "We have determined on applying to the present
Congress for a renewal of the Charter of the Bank," he informed
an ally in early 1832. "To this course I have made up my mind
after great reflection and with the clearest conviction of its propriety." As before, Biddle professed disinterest in the politics of
the matter. "Neither I nor any of my associates have anything
whatever to do with the President or his election. I know nothing
about it and care nothing about it. The Bank has never had any
concern in elections; it will not have any now." Jackson might
stand or fall. "The Bank cares not. . . . It takes it own time and
its own way." Yet having said this, Biddle judged that Jackson
would be "ten times more disposed" to veto renewal after reelection than before. And if he did veto before the election, he must
surely incur the wrath of the people. "Even I, who do not feel the
slightest interest in him, would be sorry to ascribe to a President
of the United States a course much fitter for a humble dema-
gogue than the Chief Magistrate of a great country."

Biddle commenced the case for renewal himself. In a letter to
Congress he described the Bank as being "connected intimately
with the local business of every section of the United States,
with the commercial interchanges between the several States,
and the intercourse of them all with foreign nations." In each of
these areas the Bank had contributed substantially to the general
welfare, and wisdom consisted in renewing its charter, that the
good work continue. Biddle acknowledged that the existing char-

ter had four years to run; his reason for applying early was to give the Bank and the myriad enterprises and individuals it served time to plan their futures.

Daniel Webster took up the Bank's case where Biddle left off. Any Senate speech by Webster was an occasion, guaranteed to pack the galleries. That this one involved a direct challenge to the Jackson administration made it all the more appealing. The "Godlike Daniel," as he was often called, drew himself up and launched forth. He praised the Bank for preserving America from unsound money. "A disordered currency is one of the greatest of political evils," he declared. "It undermines the virtues necessary for the support of the social system, and encourages propensities destructive of its happiness. It wars against industry, frugality, and economy; and it fosters the evil spirits of extravagance and speculation." Webster was known as an advocate of business, but he also had a reputation for oratorical surprise. His surprise this day was to contend that the lower classes—not the wealthy—would be the ones most damaged by the destruction of the Bank. Such an eventuality would throw the people upon the flimsy notes of unreliable state banks. "Ordinary tyranny, oppression, excessive taxation: these bear lightly upon the happiness of the mass of the community, compared with fraudulent currencies and the robberies committed by depreciated paper." The rich found ways to protect themselves against inflation; the poor simply suffered. Webster predicted that reliance on the state banks would cause gold and silver to vanish, as the state banks flooded the country with their small-denomination notes. He cited English history to make his point. "When Mr. Pitt, in the year 1797, proposed in

Parliament to authorize the Bank of England to issue one pound notes, Mr. Burke lay sick at Bath of an illness from which he never recovered. And he is said to have written to the late Mr. Canning, 'Tell Mr. Pitt that if he consents to the issuing of one pound notes, he must never expect to see a guinea again.'"

As Webster finished, Thomas Hart Benton rose to rebut. Benton's alliance with Jackson couldn't have been predicted a decade earlier, when he and Jackson took opposite sides in a shooting brawl in Nashville. Jackson's shoulder caught a bullet that spent years in his flesh before finally popping out, by which time, however, he and Benton had discovered a common devotion to the emerging democracy and a shared distrust of banks. In 1832 Benton was a senator from Missouri, and his belief that gold and silver constituted the only honest money was earning him the nickname "Old Bullion." He rejected Webster's assertion that the Bank of the United States was good for the common people of America. Conceivably the Bank's policies benefited some workers in the Northeast, he said, but the benefit of such policies came at the expense of the population of the rest of the country. "They lead to the *abduction of its gold and silver*. If notes are issued, they are payable at the branch bank"—in a given state—"and an adequate supply of gold and silver must be kept on hand to redeem them; but these orders being drawn on Philadelphia, the gold and silver of the state must be sent there to meet them." By stealing its specie, the capitalists of the northern seaboard sucked the life out of the South and West. "They gorge to repletion, then vomit their load into the vast receptacles of the Northeast, and gorge again." The honest people of the

heartland staggered under the burden of debt as the money supply contracted; the capitalists scooped up their foreclosed farms
and bankrupted shops at auctions rigged by the policies of the
Bank and its minions. The consequence was as appalling as it was
inevitable. "In these mock sales of towns and cities may be laid
the foundation for the titles and estates of our future nobility—
Duke of Cincinnati! Earl of Lexington! Marquis of Nashville!
Count of St. Louis! Prince of New Orleans! Such may be the
titles of the bank nobility. . . . Yes, sir! When the renewed charter
is brought in for us to vote upon, I shall consider myself as voting
upon a bill for the establishment of *lords and commons* in this
America, and for the eventual establishment of a *King!*"

Neither the approximate accuracy of Benton's account of the
Bank's operations nor his blatant demagoguery regarding their
portent stopped the Senate from approving renewal by a narrow
margin, or the House from backing it more enthusiastically.
Jackson was certain Biddle had bought some of the favorable
votes, though he couldn't prove it. Roger Taney, Jackson's attorney general, allowed more room for nuance. Taney recounted
how one congressman had switched to Biddle's side after receiving a generous loan from the Bank. "I do not mean to say that he
was directly bribed to give this vote," Taney wrote. "From the
character he sustained and from what I knew of him, I think he
would have resented any thing that he regarded as an attempt to
corrupt him. But he wanted the money, and felt grateful for the
favor. And perhaps he thought that an institution which was so
useful to him, and had behaved with so much kindness, could
not be injurious or dangerous to the public, and that it would be

as well to continue it."

CONGRESSIONAL APPROVAL PUT the fate of the Bank in Jackson's hands. He hadn't expected such a gift, doubting that his opponents would be so foolish as to provide him an issue on which his philosophical inclination and his political interest so clearly coincided. That Biddle could blunder this badly didn't surprise him, but he thought Clay should have realized opposition to the Bank would be an easy winner for the president. Obviously the man was desperate.

"A bank of the United States is in many respects convenient for the Government and useful to the people," Jackson acknowledged in receiving the renewal bill. This convenience, and his respect for his predecessors, had inclined him to let the Bank live out its charter, despite his stated reservations about its legitimacy. But the Bank's advocates, by seeking renewal, aimed to extend the Bank's existence. To this he could not agree. Jackson appreciated that the Supreme Court had ruled the Bank constitutional in the McCulloch case. John Marshall and the other justices were entitled to their views, he said, but these didn't bind the president. "Each public officer who takes an oath to support the Constitution swears that he will support it as he understands it, and not as it is understood by others. It is as much the duty of the House of Representatives, of the Senate, and of the President to decide upon the constitutionality of any bill or resolution which may be presented to them for passage or approval as it is of the supreme judges." This principle was sufficiently important that Jackson felt obliged to reiterate it: "The opinion of the judges has no more authority over Congress than the opinion of Congress has over the judges, and on that point the President is independent of both." Jackson read the "necessary and proper" clause of the Constitution more literally than Marshall did or Hamilton had; the Founders, he inferred, meant "necessary *and* proper," not "necessary *or* proper." As useful as a national bank might be, it was by no means necessary. It was, therefore, unconstitutional.

Jackson's view of the Constitution and its interpretation was hardly unique at the time; the doctrine of judicial supremacy remained a conceit of John Marshall and a minority in America. Yet much more was involved in the Bank question than constitutionality. Like Benton, Jackson believed the Bank undermined democracy by creating a monopoly of money. Of the Bank's twenty-five directors, only five were answerable to the people. The rest served the interests of capital. "It is easy to conceive that great evils to our country and its institutions might flow from such a concentration of power in the hands of a few men irresponsible to the people." Nor were the monopolists all Americans; almost a third of the stock of the Bank was owned by foreigners. "Is there no danger to our liberty and independence in a bank that in its nature has so little to bind it to our country?" Most to the point, the Bank eroded the equality on which democracy rested.

Distinctions in society will always exist under every just government. Equality of talents, of education, or of wealth can not be produced by human institutions. . . . But when the laws undertake to add to these natural and just advantages artificial distinctions, to grant title, gratuities, and exclusive privileges, to make the rich richer and the potent more powerful, the humble members of society—the farmers, mechanics, and laborers—who have neither the time nor the means of securing like favors to themselves, have a right to complain of the injustice of their Government. There are no necessary evils in government. Its evils exist only in its abuses. If it would confine itself to equal protection and, as Heaven does its rains, shower its favors alike on the high and the low, the rich and the poor, it would be an unqualified blessing.

Because the Bank conferred its favors preferentially, it defeated the purposes of democratic government. The renewal bill required a veto and accordingly received it.

THE REACTION TO Jackson's Bank veto was instantaneous and sharp. "A more deranging, radical, law-upsetting document was never promulgated by the wildest Roman fanatic," a New England editor declared. "Let it be remembered that every military chieftain—Sylla, Caesar, Cromwell—all have obtained unlimited and despotic power by pretending to be the sole friends of the People and often by denouncing the rich, and by cajoling the poor with prospects which they never intended to be realized, or only realized with chains and slavery and dungeons, or enrollment in the legions assembled to add to the power of the tyrant." The share price of Bank stock plummeted, as did the price of commodities. Construction projects were suspended; steamboats stayed at the wharf. Protesters took to the streets in several cities and towns. Those in Philadelphia, the home of the Bank, declared their "astonishment, indignation, and alarm" that the president would so upset the economy and trifle with the national interest. The Philadelphia protesters went on to demand the defeat of Jackson in the election now but months away.

This last demand revealed the reason for the intensity of the reaction. Jackson's veto was neither unexpected (he had long been saying he opposed renewal) nor immediately significant (the existing charter had four years left to run). But the protesters aimed to marshal the anger at the veto and use it remove Jackson from office in favor of the capital-friendly Clay.

Biddle thought the veto guaranteed Jackson's defeat. "I am delighted with it," he wrote Clay regarding the veto message. "It has all the fury of a chained panther biting the bars of his cage. It is really a manifesto of anarchy. . . . My hope is that it will contribute to relieve the country from the dominion of these miserable people." Biddle now dropped his cloak of nonpartisanship, telling Clay, "You are destined to be the instrument of that deliverance." He paid to distribute Clay's speeches and provided other financial and logistical support. "At no period of your life has the country ever had a deeper stake in you," he wrote Clay. "I wish you success most cordially, because I believe the institutions of the Union are involved in it."

Jackson couldn't have been happier at the uproar or at Biddle's opposition. The capitalists were powerful, but the democrats (many of whom now called themselves Democrats) were more numerous. "The veto works well everywhere," he wrote with satisfaction as election day neared. "It has put down the Bank instead of prostrating me."

Jackson's assessment proved the more accurate. In the election he increased his popular majority from 1828 and routed Clay in the electoral college by 219 to 49. The lesson seemed clear, at least to the Jacksonians: when democracy and capitalism collided at the ballot box, democracy won.

BIDDLE HAD KNOWN he was taking a risk in hitching the Bank to Clay. But he considered himself and the Bank impregnable. For all Jackson's opposition, the Bank still held the government's deposits, which gave the Bank its great leverage. Jackson and the democrats would never touch these, for in doing so they would bring the temple down upon their own heads. "They will not *dare* to remove them," Biddle told Webster. "If the deposits are withdrawn, it will be a declaration of war which cannot be recalled."

Biddle fatally underestimated Jackson. The president learned of Biddle's defiance; he also heard that Biddle and the Bank were plotting another contraction of credit. "This operation will be performed under the avowed idea that it is necessary and preliminary to winding up its concerns," Jackson's informant told him. The contraction would cause a run on state banks, which would be forced to suspend specie payments. "The immense injury to the whole nation resulting from that event, it is believed, and not without foundation, will induce a strong public feeling in favor of recharter of the Bank as the only means of restoring a sound currency."

Jackson determined to preempt Biddle by going straight for

the deposits. He enlisted Attorney General Taney to prepare the legal brief for removal, and he dispatched confidant Amos Kendall to sound out state banks across the country to see if they were willing to accept the deposits and provide the services currently furnished by Biddle's Bank. This was no idle question, for though the state banks could use the business, many feared to cross Biddle. Kendall discovered that the closer to Philadelphia the banks were, the greater their fear. "Most of the banks here will answer precisely as the Bank of the United States desires," he wrote Jackson from Baltimore. Boston's bankers were bolder, to the point of offering their personal pledges for the security of the government's deposits. Yet even the bold ones declared that if Jackson were to act, he must do so decisively and at once. Biddle would surely retaliate against any bank that went along with the administration, and if the cooperating bank were caught short of cash, it would be ruined. Kendall summarized the feeling: "*Immediate removal* or *no removal.*"

Biddle's spies in the banking world apprised him of Jackson's planning, and he plotted his response. "The real sin of the Bank in the eyes of the Executive," he told a colleague, "is that it is refractory and unmanageable. When these people first came into power . . . they considered the Bank a part of the spoil." Biddle had refused to yield to the Jacksonian efforts to sweep the Bank into democratic politics. "We saw all that would follow from the slightest concession, and determined, since there must be war, to begin it in the frontiers by letting them know they were to have nothing to do with the Bank." Biddle was referring to the earlier credit contraction in the West, which he now admitted had backfired against the Bank. "From that time they resolved that as they could not bend it they would break it." Biddle prepared a new approach. "In half an hour, I can remove all the constitutional scruples in the District of Columbia. Half a dozen Presidencies"—of Bank branches—"a dozen cashierships, fifty clerkships, a hundred directorships to worthy friends who have no character and no money." While deciding which public officials to bribe, Biddle braced himself for whatever Jackson might do. "We must go on to the end of the chapter," he said.

In September 1833 Jackson struck the blow. He convened a special Cabinet session and told the secretaries he was going to withdraw the deposits at once. He hurried through the constitutional arguments against the Bank, preferring to take his stand on the morality of the contest. The fight against the Bank was part of the historic struggle for liberty, he declared. Kings and tyrants had fallen, yet the battle continued. "The mass of the people have more to fear from combinations of the wealthy and professional classes—from an aristocracy which through the influence of riches and talents, insidiously employed, sometimes succeeds in preventing political institutions, however well adjusted, from securing the freedom of the citizen." Biddle's Bank had gained "almost entire dominion over the circulating medium, and with it, power to increase or diminish the price of property and to levy taxes on the people in the shape of premiums and interest." The Founders had fought to free Americans from such arbitrary rule. To continue the fight was the current generation's "sacred duty."

BIDDLE'S SPIES INFORMED him of Jackson's decision even before the president announced it. Biddle counterattacked instantly. He called in more loans, additionally tightened credit, and generally made money scarce. In response to questions he said he was simply steadying the Bank against the uncertainty the president's rash move had precipitated. But he took few pains to hide the larger goal: to demonstrate the need for a national bank beyond the reach of politics. Meanwhile he went ahead with his bribery plan, conferring directorships and other plums on Jackson allies who agreed to defect.

Biddle's assault on the money supply produced the pain he desired. Samuel Swartout, Jackson's director of the New York customhouse, resisted a Biddle bribe but wrote the Bank chief of the terrible injury the current money pressure was inflicting on the financial markets. "It is dreadful here," Swartout declared, "and no hope of relief except through your institution. You must be *liberal.* . . . The old friends and dependents of the Bank are perishing for want of aid. Surely the institution cannot mean this?" Biddle had proved his point, Swartout said. "Now that the effect of the late measure"—the withdrawal of the deposits—"has been made manifest, you can relieve the whole community. . . . Rely upon it, you would receive due credit and consideration for it. I speak to you, my dear sir, with the freedom of a friend. Would to God the Bank would take a noble, liberal course and thus justify itself to the world. . . . Its power has been shown; now let its mercy be manifested."

Biddle was in no mood for mercy. He tightened the

screws still more. The panic spread from New York to Boston
and Philadelphia. Banks collapsed under the strain, leaving
depositors empty-handed. "My view is simply this," Biddle
wrote the director of the Bank branch at Boston. "The ties of
party allegiance can only be broken by the actual conviction of
existing distress in the community. Nothing but the evidence
of suffering abroad will produce any effect in Congress. If the
Bank remains strong and quiet, the course of events will save
the Bank and save all the institutions which are now in great
peril." The Bank must not relent. "If from too great a sensitive-
ness, from the fear of offending or the desire of conciliating, the
Bank permits itself to be frightened or coaxed into any relaxation
of its present measures, the relief will itself be cited as evidence
that the measures of the Government are not injurious or oppressive, and the Bank will inevitably be prostrated. Our only safety
is in pursuing a steady course of firm restriction." Courage would
bring victory, though not at once. "I have no doubt that such a
course will ultimately lead to restoration of the currency and the
recharter of the Bank. How soon this will take place, it is of
course difficult to conjecture."

It grew more difficult in subsequent weeks. "The future is
full of gloom and confusion," Biddle wrote in February 1834.
Yet the uncertainty made him more determined. "My own
course is decided. All the other banks and all the merchants
may break, but the Bank of the United States shall not break."
A Biddle uncle had been an officer in the Continental Navy. "I
have asked Commodore Biddle what is the least sail under
which a man of war can lie to in a gale of wind, and he says a

close-reefed main top sail. So our squadron will be put under close-reefed main top sails and ride out the gale for the next two years. As to those who have no sea room and breakers under their lee, they must rely on Providence." Jackson didn't know whom he was tangling with. "The worthy President thinks that because he has scalped Indians . . . he is to have his way with the Bank. He is mistaken. . . . He may as well send at once and engage lodgings in Arabia."

BIDDLE'S WILLINGNESS AND ability to ravage the economy confirmed Jackson's judgment of the malignant irresponsibility of the moneyed class. It was precisely this power of the Bank that had determined Jackson to destroy it. And he remained determined to do so, regardless of the pain the destruction produced. "Were all the worshipers of the golden calf to memorialise me and request a restoration of the deposits," he said to Martin Van Buren, "I would cut my right hand from my body before I would do such an act. The golden calf may be worshiped by others, but as for myself I will serve the Lord." Jackson was certain he was serving the Lord—and democracy—in holding out against Biddle. "My conscience told me it was right to stop the career of this destroying monster. I took the step fearlessly, believing it a duty I owed to my God and my country."

Jackson told himself the pain was localized in the groups that most deserved it. "There is no real general distress," he wrote confidentially. "It is only with those who live by borrowing, trade on loans, and the gamblers in stocks. . . . It would be a godsend to society if all such were put down."

The distress in fact was more general than Jackson allowed, as he might have inferred upon receiving a petition from six thousand bankers, brokers, and merchants requesting relief. But the president refused to reconsider. "Relief, sir!" he thundered to a quaking spokesman for the petitioners. "Come not to me, sir! Go to the monster! . . . Go to Nicholas Biddle. We have no money here. . . . Biddle has all the money. He has millions of specie in his vaults at this moment, lying idle, and yet you come to *me* to save you from breaking. . . . It is folly, sir, to talk to Andrew Jackson. The government will not bow to the monster."

For Jackson, as for Biddle, the contest had become supremely personal. "The Bank, Mr. Van Buren, is trying to kill me," he told the vice president. *"But I will kill it!"*

AND HE DID. Biddle's friends in Congress deserted him one by one as it became apparent that the public was blaming him, not Jackson, for the panic. Henry Clay convinced the Senate that Jackson required censure, but the House, whose members all faced the voters imminently, fled Biddle and the Bank. Biddle relented under the political duress, easing the panic, but the action did him no good, as it demonstrated that he could have eased things earlier.

The congressional campaign of 1834 was the stormiest in memory. In Philadelphia mobs rioted against the Bank and against Biddle, forcing the Bank chief to barricade himself in his home, surrounded by armed guards. He and his family survived, but the

Whigs—as the party of capital now called itself—almost did not. So severe was the Whig defeat that even the formerly most Bank-friendly Whigs turned their backs on Biddle. "There is one cause of congratulation connected with the result of the recent election, in which even *we* can participate," Thurlow Weed, the leader of the New York Whigs, said. "It has terminated the United States Bank war. . . . After staggering along from year to year with a doomed bank upon our shoulders, both the bank and our party are overwhelmed. The burden, however, is now removed."

Biddle continued to plot desultorily with the Bank's few remaining friends against Jackson and his heir apparent, Van Buren. Daniel Webster urged Biddle to employ his money and influence against the Democrats in critical districts. Yet Webster too insisted on keeping a public distance from Biddle. "You will of course *burn this,* and let no eye but your own see it," he concluded one letter to the Bank president. The next letter ended simply, *"Burn."*

Nothing came of Biddle's plots. He muttered against the "gang of banditti" in the executive branch but was forced to watch their new chief march to victory in the 1836 election. Meanwhile, as the Bank's federal charter ran out, Biddle sought a new legal home for the institution, which Pennsylvania obligingly provided. The Bank of the United States slipped into history, but the Bank of the United States of Pennsylvania, shorn of the earlier bank's inter-state branches and deprived of the federal patronage, yet housed in the same marble temple on Chestnut Street, carried on.

This was a minor victory for Biddle; a somewhat larger one, albeit merely moral, came months later. Jackson's defeat of Biddle and the Bank restored what the Jacksonians hoped would be democratic control of the money supply, but in fact it left the money supply even more at the mercy of the capitalists than before. The hundreds of state banks, now freed of the oversight of the Bank of the United States, issued bank notes profligately, producing speculative bubbles in all manner of commodities and property. Jackson could do nothing about most of the speculation, but he could curb that in land, and he did so by issuing a "specie circular" in July 1836 directing federal officers to accept only gold and silver in exchange for public lands.

The measure dampened the speculation in land, but it simultaneously disordered the money system. Specie flowed to the West, the locale of the land sales, and away from the East, the hub of the country's economic activity. An eastern banker exaggerated, but only a little, when he said of the specie directive, "It transferred specie from the place where it was most wanted, in order to sustain the general currency of the country, to places where it was not wanted at all." Another observer remarked, "The monetary affairs of the whole country were convulsed—millions upon millions of coin were *in transitu* in every direction and consequently withdrawn from useful employment. Specie was going up and down the same river to and from the South and North and East and West at the same time."

Amid the domestic financial disturbance arrived a shock from abroad. The speculation in America had been part of a transatlantic boom, and at almost the same time that Jackson was issuing his specie circular, the Bank of England raised interest rates and broadly tightened credit. Cotton prices fell on British markets, and because the American South was Britain's principal supplier, the falling prices punished American planters and their brokers. Several firms collapsed in New Orleans, and then in New York, at which point the growing anxiety became a wholesale panic.

Nicholas Biddle blamed Jackson and democracy for the country's financial woes, and he thought the masses were getting what they deserved. "The crusade against banks and the discrimination at the Land Offices between specie and bank paper has not been without its effect on the less intelligent part of our population," Biddle declared. He couldn't help gloating at the Democrats' discomfiture, even though it devastated the economy and threatened to swamp his own bank.

Biddle retired in 1839, claiming ill health but secretly planning a candidacy for president. He must have been sicker than he knew, for though 1840 proved a good year for the party of cap-

Andrew Jackson holding aloft the order for the removal of the federal deposits from the second Bank of the United States. As the Bank collapses, the directors flee for their lives. Nicholas Biddle is the one with horns.

ital, Biddle was delusional in thinking Americans would elect a
man best known as a bank president to be their own president.
Instead they elected William Henry Harrison, like Jackson a former general but unlike him a Whig. No one paid the least attention to Biddle.

He suffered another blow when his old bank collapsed amid
scandal in 1841. Charles Dickens visited Philadelphia a short
while later, reaching the city at night. "Looking out of my chamber window before going to bed," he wrote, "I saw, on the opposite side of the way, a handsome building of white marble, which
had a mournful ghost-like aspect, dreary to behold. I attributed
this to the sombre influence of the night, and on rising in the
morning looked out again, expecting to see its steps and portico
thronged with groups of people passing in and out. The door
was still tight shut, however; the same cold, cheerless air pre-
vailed. . . . I hastened to inquire its name and purpose. . . . It was
the Tomb of many fortunes, the Great Catacomb of investment,
the memorable United States Bank."

3

The Bonds of Union

On the tour that took him to Philadelphia, Charles Dickens traveled by steamboat and train, two modes of transportation that hadn't existed when Nicholas Biddle was a boy. The steamboat came first, turning American transportation almost on its head by allowing river traffic to flow expeditiously uphill for the first time in history. From 1807, when Robert Fulton's *Clermont* made the journey from New York up the Hudson to Albany, through the 1850s, by which time steamboats on the Mississippi had become floating palaces, the steamboat transformed the American economy. It greatly accelerated the development of the interior of North America, as trade between that region and the eastern seaboard became genuinely reciprocal. The western frontier of settlement leapfrogged the Mississippi Valley; the entire basin filled rapidly with people. The opening of the Erie Canal in 1825 amplified the steamboat's impact by making near neighbors of Albany and Buffalo, which heretofore had been separated by three thousand river and ocean miles for anyone interested in transporting goods in bulk. The Great Lakes became the backyard of New York City; the whole eastern half of the continent drew together in a single network of trade.

The net grew tighter and its mesh finer in the 1830s and 1840s with the introduction of railroads. Railroads were even more revolutionary for transport than steamboats, for while the latter were confined to the routes God had created—the Erie and most other canals being too small for steamboats, and permitting only mule-drawn barges—the former could go wherever human will, human strength, and the capitalist imagination collaborated to direct them. Railroads linked cities to cities, cities to towns, and towns to farms. Railroads magnified the commerce of existing cities and allowed the creation of new cities. Chicago was founded where a canal connected Lake Michigan to the Mississippi's drainage system, but the astonishing growth it experienced during the mid-nineteenth century reflected the arrival of the railroad. Formerly weeks from New York, Chicago now was just days distant, and the railroads that fanned out from Chicago made it the queen of the prairies and the gateway to the Northwest.

The revolution in transport effected by the steamboat and the railroad made possible other revolutions. One involved the expansion of markets: of the arenas where goods were bought and sold. Markets had existed from time out of mind, located wherever persons exchanged one commodity for another. But they were limited by existing transportation technology; farmers might travel half a day each week carrying crops to market, but they couldn't afford to spend much more time than that on the road. Steamboats and railroads, which slashed transport costs nine-tenths or more, freed farmers and other producers to send their goods much farther. Markets grew in size and sophistication; they melded and merged. New York dominated the Atlantic seaboard, Chicago and St. Louis the interior of the country, New Orleans the Gulf of Mexico. By the mid-nineteenth century it became possible—and economically necessary—to talk about national markets in wheat, cotton, corn, and certain other basic products.

The revolutions in transport and markets combined—with the help of advances in steam technology—to inaugurate the industrial revolution in America. Steam engines powered looms in textile factories, rollers in flour mills, stamp presses in mines and metalworking shops; but it was the prospect of easy transport and broad markets for the products of the industrial process that inspired investors to risk their capital on the new equipment and techniques. Of those investors who took the plunge, some surfaced without their shirts; but others succeeded beyond the wildest dreams of anyone since Croesus.

NICHOLAS BIDDLE DIED in 1844, "heart-broken," a friend said, at the demise of the bank he had guarded so jealously. Andrew Jackson died the following year, convinced that in besting Biddle he had saved democracy from moneyed tyranny. But something else distracted Jackson in his final hours: the annexation of Texas, toward which he had worked for many years. The delay in Jackson's success was due not least to John Quincy Adams, who had warned that taking Texas would precipitate a war with Mexico, its previous owner and continuing claimant.

Events proved Adams right when hostilities commenced in 1846, and he went to his grave in 1848 confirmed in his perspicacity and convinced of the folly of his country's course.

That course appeared less foolish when news arrived in the East, not long after Adams's death, that gold had been discovered in California, part of the prize of the Mexican War. The gold discovery set off a rush to California and resulted in the extraction of hundreds of millions of dollars of gold from California's mines in the next decade, and of billions of dollars of gold in the decades after that from mines discovered by prospectors instructed by the California example.

The discoveries came at a crucial moment for the American and world economies. The transport, market, and industrial revolutions were not merely American phenomena; similar developments occurred in several countries of Western Europe. What all required, besides technical innovation, was financial liquidity. At the midpoint of the nineteenth century, the money system inherited from the pre-industrial age was braking economic expansion; what the world needed was a new system, one combining stability with the capacity to underwrite rapid growth.

What it got was the flood of gold from California, Australia, and elsewhere. Gold had long been the money of choice for investors, being beyond the ability of politicians or other humans to produce and consequently devalue. But there had always been too little of it—which was why silver, paper, and other items were substituted. The infusion of gold—by some estimates, as much gold was dug from the ground in the quarter-century after the California discovery as had been unearthed in the previous three hundred years—enabled the major trading states to embrace the yellow metal as their sole monetary standard. The British led the way into this new golden age, and Britain's gold standard became the model for other nations, which one by one abandoned silver and paper. By the beginning of the twentieth century nearly all the world's trading states did their business in gold.

The United States was one of the last to place whole faith in gold. This tardiness reflected ultimately the politics of the money question but initially the politics of the slavery question. The discovery of gold in California peopled that Pacific district far sooner than anyone had expected, and it compelled Congress to confront an issue it had been putting off: the status of slavery in the western territories. An 1850 compromise resulted in the admission of California as a free state, which angered the South, but also the opening of rest of the Mexican cession to slavery and the adoption of a stiffer fugitive slave law, which outraged the North. Each side nursed its grievances until 1854, when another compromise encouraged slaveholders and abolitionists to fight for the future of Kansas. They did so with murderous effect. A bloody-handed veteran of the Kansas conflict, John Brown, went east and in 1859 attempted to start a slave uprising in Virginia. The effort failed and Brown was executed, but the incident so frightened the South that after Abraham Lincoln of Illinois was elected president in 1860, most of the South left the Union. Lincoln interpreted his oath of office as requiring resistance to secession, and the Civil War began.

JAY COOKE CUT his banking teeth in Nicholas Biddle's Philadelphia, working with Biddle's Pennsylvania bank amid the currency derangements that followed Jackson's specie circular. Cooke was hardly more than a lad, but his very youth served him well. A contemporary still marveled, years later, at Cooke's dexterity in counting and changing bank notes.

> With lightning rapidity, the notes passed through his delicate fingers. . . . There was no hesitancy, no pause, apparently no thought or mental effort. It was as a smoothly flowing stream of noiseless water. . . . There was no counting over; one count was sufficient. . . . There was no fluster, no perturbation, no thought apparently of a mistake being possible. As he counted he could talk also. He both asked and answered questions, briefly of course, but the like I had never seen and it astonished me. I have never seen it since as Jay Cooke did it.

There was more to the lad—he wasn't yet twenty—than fast fingers. The same contemporary was arrested by Cooke's "young manly beauty . . . tall, slender, light-haired, blue-eyed, fair-complexioned, and of radiant countenance. . . . Brightness and cheerfulness characterized his whole personality. Every movement, every step, every motion of hand and arm, was a bright one."

Cooke's employer was E. W. Clark & Company, a latecomer to banking but for that reason more nimble than some older firms. Clark sold bonds for the independent Republic of Texas prior to its annexation to the Union; Cooke's inside perspective persuaded him that many of the annexation ayes in Congress represented

bondholders who wanted to ensure the security of their investment. Clark & Company sold bonds for the United States government during the war with Mexico, teaching Cooke new methods
of financing a modern, far-flung conflict. "Our firm had a branch
office in St. Louis," he recalled, "and we proceeded to sell
exchange on Philadelphia and New York at a handsome premium,
say two and a half or three percent, and with interest dating from
the hour of deposit in the St. Louis subtreasury"—a branch office
of the federal Treasury. "The mails were sometimes from ten to
fifteen days in transit"—during which time Clark & Company
received interest on funds it hadn't yet delivered. Robert J.
Walker, the Treasury secretary, caught on to the float scheme and
began demanding deposit of funds in the subtreasury closest to
the home of the bidder. "I have no doubt Robert J. remarked to
himself, 'Now that will fix those smart fellows at
E. W. Clark & Company,'" Cooke remembered. "But lo, when
the bids were opened, our share was allotted to E. W. Clark &
Brothers of St. Louis. . . . So we victimized him again."

Cooke remained with Clark & Company through the flush
times of the California gold rush, which afforded the banking
industry an entirely new arena of activity, and into the shakeout
that inevitably followed. Speculation in mining stocks led
California branches of eastern banks to overextend; when the
mining bubble burst it flattened San Francisco and sent gale
winds over the Sierra Nevada and across the continent. New
York might have withstood the tempest had a real hurricane off
Cape Hatteras not sunk a ship, the *Central America,* carrying
California gold that was to have bolstered the spirits of the Wall

Street bankers. When the ship went down, so did the hopes of averting a panic. Banks and brokers with decades of experience crumbled. "Money is not *tight*," Edward Clark wrote. "It is *not to be had at all*. No money, no confidence and no value to anything." Clark & Company was a casualty of the crash, and Jay Cooke found himself out of work.

He had tucked away enough to consider retirement, though he wasn't forty years old. And for a few years he merely dabbled. But as the nation moved toward civil war, he spotted opportunities he couldn't resist, and at the beginning of 1861 he and brother-in-law William Moorhead opened the firm of Jay Cooke & Company, headquartered at 114 South Third Street in Philadelphia.

An early venture was the sale of Pennsylvania war bonds worth $3 million and paying six percent interest. Pennsylvania's credit was dubious at this point on account of profligate previous spending. The legislature nonetheless stipulated that the bonds be sold at par or better. The banking community advised the governor that this was absurd; if the bonds couldn't be sold at a discount, they'd never sell. Cooke dissented, offering to sell the entire lot at par. To the chagrin of the others, he convinced the governor and, with the older house of Drexel & Company, won the right to sell the bonds.

He thereupon launched an advertising campaign that played to the head and heart at once. "The subscribers . . . respectfully appeal to the patriotism and State pride of Pennsylvanians in this hour of trial, that they come forward and manifest their love of the Commonwealth. . . . But independent of any motives of patriotism, there are considerations of self-interest which may be considered. . . . It is a six per cent loan, free from any taxation whatever. . . . Bidders can have the privilege of taking certificates of $50, $100, $500, $1,000 or larger sums." The law authorizing the loan guaranteed its "economical and judicious expenditure," and a special tax ensured prompt payment of interest and certain repayment of principal.

Cooke's campaign succeeded brilliantly. Individuals and institutions bought the bonds as quickly as Cooke could hand them over. He cannily published the names of all these patriots in the local papers, and sent copies across the country. He even dispatched a copy to Jefferson Davis, telling the Confederate president in a cover letter that this was what he was up against: the mobilized money of the North.

Cooke congratulated himself profusely. "It is regarded as an achievement as great as or greater than Napoleon's crossing the Alps," he wrote his brother in June 1861. "It is indeed a glorious work, and I am proud of it."

A MONTH LATER Union forces and Confederates converged on Manassas Junction, Virginia, just south of the Bull Run River. A lack of seriousness marked the Union preparations for battle; many of the troops had enlisted for a mere ninety days, reflecting the belief of their leaders that the war wouldn't last longer than that. Journalists, members of Congress, and sightseers rode horses and carriages out of Washington to observe the clash, in much the mood that took them to the circus or county fairs when

they were at home. The Union troops got the better of the early
fighting that day, but the Confederates, led by a bearded cavalry
colonel named J. E. B. Stuart and a dour former professor named
Thomas Jackson, whose stubborn demeanor caused a comrade
to liken him to a stone wall, counterattacked with a ferocity that
astonished even themselves. They shrieked as they surged forward. "There is nothing like it on this side of the infernal region,"
a Union soldier said of the rebel yell. "The peculiar corkscrew
sensation that it sends down your backbone under these circumstances can never be told. You have to feel it." The Northerners
also felt the force of the Southern bullets and artillery shells, and
fled in disorder. "The further they ran, the more frightened they
grew," wrote one of those sightseeing congressmen. "We called to
them, tried to tell them there was no danger, called them to stop,
implored them to stand. We called them cowards, denounced
them in the most offensive terms, put out our heavy revolvers
and threatened to shoot them, but all in vain. A cruel, crazy, mad,
hopeless panic possessed them."

Till now most Northerners had expected that a show of force,
a demonstration that the South wouldn't be allowed to secede in
peace, would suffice to suppress the insurrection. The battle of
Bull Run, or Manassas, as the Confederates called it, shattered
this illusion. Some Northerners swung to the other extreme,
declaring that the South should be allowed to go to hell in its
own way. A larger number, after the shock wore off, settled in for
the long war almost none had anticipated.

At this point the question of finance arose. The federal budget
had been strained before the war began. Tariffs constituted

Washington's chief source of revenue, but depressed consumption following the panic of 1857 sent the budget deep into deficit. (Whatever their other financial shortcomings, the Jacksonians had been good stewards of the budget, paying off the federal debt and typically running surpluses.) So dire was the situation by 1861 that some observers accused the Treasury secretary, Howell Cobb of Georgia, of deliberately disordering federal finances as secession approached. Cobb's fellow Southerners didn't deny it. Alexander Stephens, vice president of the Confederacy, laughingly recalled the reaction of Georgia senator Robert Toombs to Cobb's policies: "Toombs never lets Cobb pass without giving him a lick. The other night in high glee he told him in company that he had done more for secession than any other man. He had deprived the enemy of the sinews of war and left him without a dollar in the Treasury." This was hardly an exaggeration. John Sherman of Ohio, the chairman of the House Ways and Means Committee (and the brother of Union general William Tecumseh Sherman), told his colleagues in the House in December 1860 that the federal government lacked the money to pay their salaries.

Things got worse. British capitalists, tied closely to the cotton economy of the South, pulled back from the North. Specie did what specie does in crisis: it fled abroad and into hiding. Investors withheld judgment—that is, withheld their money— till they knew whether they were dealing with one nation and sovereign government or two (or several, given the Confederacy's reversion to the constitutional model of the Articles of Confederation). Had the war been short, this wouldn't have mattered much. The American economy would have recovered, government revenues revived, and the federal budget been brought back into balance. But a long war threatened grave damage. Revenues would remain depressed from the disruption to trade and hence tariffs, and spending would soar, on the bullets, bayonets, bread, and bandages the soldiers required.

During the grim season that followed Bull Run, Treasury secretary Salmon Chase of Ohio pondered his options. Chase knew little about finance, having been chosen less to balance the budget than to balance the Cabinet geographically, and to offset the ambitions of William Seward, the secretary of state, whose White House hopes had been frustrated by Lincoln but who still imagined himself the foremost of Republicans. Lincoln believed in embracing his rivals, the better to watch them.

Chase's initial proposal was a federal income tax, the first in American history. The absence of such a tax till then reflected the political consideration that it would have been unpopularly intrusive, reminding Americans why they had revolted against Britain; the economic consideration that it would have been ineffective, given that most Americans made their living from farming and had little cash income to tax; and the legal consideration that it would have been unconstitutional, violating the clause prohibiting direct taxes except when apportioned by population. But the Civil War itself was intrusive, and the added intrusion of an income tax seemed small compared to tearing young men from their homes and families and sending them off to die. An income tax promised to be increasingly effective as more Americans moved from farming to commerce and manufacturing. And in wartime the Constitution often gets bruised. As things happened, the income tax would be among the least of the insults to America's fundamental law.

In any case, Congress—dominated by Republicans after the departure of the South and all its Democrats—approved Chase's proposal, and Lincoln signed the tax bill into law. The measure was modest, affecting annual incomes only of $800 or more (at a time when the average worker earned less than $100), and those at the rate of three percent. But it opened a revenue door that helped keep the Union solvent (and set a precedent for future generations of tax men).

Another measure was hardly less revolutionary, despite being a throwback. The extraordinary expenses of the first year of the war far outstripped the government's gold reserves, forcing it in December 1861 to suspend specie payments—that is, to stop redeeming short-term notes in gold. In essence this put the government on a paper standard, which Chase proposed to formalize. The government would issue fiat money and require creditors to accept it.

The proposal evoked scorn in certain quarters. A few really old timers recited the phrase "not worth a Continental" from the fiat-money era of the American Revolution, and opponents of paper saw no reason to expect better now. "The wit of man has never discovered a means by which paper currency can be kept at par value except by its speedy, cheap, certain convertibility into gold and silver," Ohio congressman George Pendleton declared. "Prices will be inflated. . . . Incomes will depreciate. The savings of the poor will vanish. The hoardings of the widow will melt

away. Bonds, mortgages, and notes . . . will lose their value."
Other opponents called the measure unconstitutional. The
Founders knew the difference between hard cash and flimsy, the
constitutional objectors asserted; this was why they had allowed
Congress to "coin" money but not to print it. Still other opponents invoked Providence. "Gold and silver are the only true
measure of value," a devout banker declared. "These metals were
prepared by the Almighty for this very purpose."

The advocates of paper money argued just as passionately.
Congressman William Kellogg of Illinois contended that the
present crisis was but another episode in the long struggle
between democracy and capitalism. "I am pained when I sit in
my place in the House and hear members talk about the sacred-
ness of capital," he said. "They will vote six hundred thousand of
the flower of the American youth for the army to be sacrificed
without a blush. But the great interests of capital, of currency,
must not be touched." Kellogg thought it time to draft money.
"We have summoned the youth; they have come. I would sum-
mon the capital, and if it does not come voluntarily, before this
republic shall go down or one star be lost, I would take every cent
. . . from the treasury of capitalists . . . and press it into the use
of the government."

Chase didn't propose to settle the constitutional debate (he
would work on that after the war, when he became chief justice
of the Supreme Court). Nor did he wish to weigh in on the question of democracy versus capitalism. Rather he pleaded straight-
forward necessity. "Immediate action is of great importance," he
told Congress in February 1862. "The Treasury is nearly empty."

Which of the arguments persuaded the most members of Congress is hard to know. But majorities in both houses agreed that paper was necessary, and after carving out exceptions for interest on federal bonds (which the government had to pay in gold) and for customs duties (which merchants had to pay in gold), they gave Chase what he wanted. At the end of February, Lincoln signed the Legal Tender Act into law.

Bankers, creditors, and others with an interest in a sound currency feared the worst. The difference in value between gold and the greenbacks grew steadily. Before 1862 ended 134 greenback dollars were required to buy 100 gold dollars. In 1863 the price rose to 172. In 1864 it reached 285. The fate of the greenback tracked the fate of the Union armies. When they lost, so did the greenback; when they rallied, the greenbacks did too. So close was the connection that speculators betting on a fall in the greenback—that is, a rise in the price of gold—could be heard whistling "Dixie" on Wall Street, while the theme song of those anticipating a rise in the greenback hummed "John Brown's Body."

The eventual success of Union arms was one factor keeping the greenback from spiraling down into nothingness; an overhaul of the federal tax code was another. The 1861 income tax turned out to have been just the start; the Internal Revenue Act of 1862 added taxes on alcohol and tobacco, playing cards and billiard tables, carriages and yachts, medicines and advertisements, manufactures and processed farm goods, licenses and stamps, dividends and inheritances. The earlier income tax was raised and expanded.

All the taxes helped keep the Northern economy from overheating; they also demonstrated the government's seriousness in paying for the war by honest means rather than merely issuing paper. The result—despite further resorts to paper, to a wartime total of nearly $450 million—was that the Union was spared the ruinous inflation of the Revolutionary War (and of the Confederacy, where no such discipline was practiced). At the end of the war, the Northern cost of living was a modest (for wartime) seventy-five percent higher than it had been at the beginning.

THERE WAS ANOTHER secret to the Union's solvency: Jay Cooke. Before the war Cooke's politics hadn't extended beyond Pennsylvania, but his family's had. His brother Henry D. Cooke owned the leading Republican newspaper in Ohio and had supported Salmon Chase as governor and then senator of that state and John Sherman as congressman. Henry D. plumped Chase for Treasury secretary and Sherman for his replacement as senator; when both appointments came through, Jay Cooke urged his brother to move east, that they might capitalize on the connections. "Can't you sell out the papers and open a banking house in Washington?" Jay asked. "At least can't you inaugurate something whereby we can all safely make some cash?" The brothers' father seconded the advice. "H. D.'s plan in getting Chase into the Cabinet and Sherman into the Senate is accomplished," he said. "Now is the time for making money. . . . The door is open."

Together the brothers stepped through. "I have talked with Sherman, who is on the Finance Committee in the Senate,"

Henry wrote Jay. "He will help us as far as in his power. He will be the leading spirit of the Committee, and his aid will be invaluable." Henry apprised Chase of Jay's expertise and patriotism, and on the strength of the recommendation Chase offered Jay a position as assistant treasurer. "It is an office of great responsibility," Chase wrote Jay. It didn't pay as much as Cooke could earn in the private sector, but in a war all made sacrifices.

Cooke declined the job, deeming the sacrifice too great. Yet he did support the Union, and he watched anxiously, from the distance of Philadelphia, as the Union and Confederate forces faced off for the battle of Bull Run. Among those most interested in the outcome of the contest were speculators in government bonds and other securities, who had sent their own agents to the front to report back as soon as the battle was decided. In their haste to be first, some of those agents left amid the early Union success and told of a great victory for the North. The real story— that the Union had lost the battle—required hours to overtake the hasty reports, as the fastest-riding agents were long gone, the slower ones were slowed further by the confusion of the Union retreat, and the government censored telegraph traffic. Not till the next day—Monday—did the news reach Philadelphia that the Union had suffered a stunning setback.

Jay Cooke's response combined Union patriotism and capitalist opportunism. He walked from his Third Street office around the business district of Philadelphia, persuading his colleagues in finance and his customers in commerce and manufacturing to contribute to the war effort. Within hours he sold nearly $2 million in short-term government notes. He made no commission on the sale, but it didn't require much imagination to think that he might make a commission on future sales should a formal arrangement with the Treasury be established.

The Philadelphians' $2 million was welcome, yet it was hardly more than a gesture at a moment when Union expenses for the war were approaching $1 million per day. And though Chase's monetary and fiscal reforms would underpin the war effort over the long term, the Union government required immediate cash to keep its army in the field. Chase invited Cooke to join him in appealing to the financial communities of New York and Boston in the same way Cooke had appealed to Philadelphia. Boston cooperated readily enough, but New York was a hard sell. Throughout the war New York would be notorious for its apathy—at times violent antipathy—toward the war effort; this shortfall of Union patriotism was exacerbated in the financial community by the international connections of many of New York's bankers, whose foreign partners had no emotional stake in the Americans' fight. Chase and Cooke spoke to the New Yorkers' national pride, and then to their pecuniary interest. By one account Chase threatened to bury New York in paper if the bond sale failed. "I hope you will find that you can take the loans required," he said. "If not, I must go back to Washington and issue notes for circulation. For, gentlemen, the war must go on until this rebellion is put down, if we have to put out paper until it takes a thousand dollars to buy a breakfast."

The New Yorkers anted up, but grudgingly. At a dinner cele- brating the successful subscription, the leader of a syndicate that included Boston and Philadelphia—the New Yorkers refused to go alone—took the floor. "Mr. Chase," he said, "you have now received from the Associated Banks the vast sum of $50 million. We all earnestly hope that this sum will be sufficient to end the war. Should it not prove enough, we wish to notify you that you cannot depend upon further aid from the Associated Banks. . . . We owe a duty to our stockholders and dare not encroach further upon their rights."

The attitude of the New Yorkers convinced Chase that in Cooke he had an ally of rare parts, a money man willing to take a broad view of self-interest, if not necessarily put self-interest aside. Cooke—like Chase—considered the Union a long-term project. Whether or not he made money on its war bonds, he would make money on its future, assuming it survived.

IN FACT HE did intend to make money on the Union war bonds. Cooke cultivated Chase assiduously, hosting the Treasury secretary at his estate outside Philadelphia. Chase brought along his daughter, Katherine, who had served as the lady of the Chase household since her mother had died. Kate Chase was the darling of wartime Washington: beautiful, outgoing, the heart's desire of all the young men who spied her on their way to the front. Jay Cooke was among the smitten. "Kate Chase spent Tuesday night with us," he wrote his brother. "She is a glorious girl." But Cooke kept his mind on business sufficiently to follow Chase when the secretary returned to Washington, leaving his daughter at Cooke's. Partner William Moorhead telegraphed Cooke to say the Philadelphia office was missing him. "It is a loss in dollars and cents to have you absent." But Moorhead reckoned Cooke knew what he was doing. "You are on a worthy mission, one that must not only result to the benefit of our worthy Uncle Sam, but some way or other to that of yourself and the house."

How to benefit Uncle Sam was easy: sell the Union bonds. How to benefit Cooke & Company was harder. Cooke spent the first several months of the war making himself useful to Chase. He sold small issues of notes, purchased gold and foreign currencies on the Treasury's behalf, and offered Chase advice on various matters. But the modest fees he earned weren't what he had in mind. "We can do the work but must be careful not to work for *honor* alone," he explained to Henry, who had opened the Washington office Jay recommended. "I can easily understand how we can purchase and deliver gold et cetera, but do not understand how we are to get *paid* for it."

In time he contrived a plan—audacious, even unheard of, yet appealing to Chase, whose frustration with the traditional bankers mounted by the month. The war grew more expensive, but the bankers, preoccupied with their profit margins, became increasingly reluctant to purchase the Treasury issues. They insisted that Chase let them buy below par, which he refused to do, believing it would evince desperation. Chase considered marketing the American bonds in Europe, only to be told by the Rothschilds' agent that any such attempt would be futile. Chase then turned to Cooke, who proposed to become the Treasury's agent. The government hoped to sell $500 million in six percent bonds that could be called in five years and matured in twenty years. Cooke said he would sell these "five-twenties" for a commission of one-half of one percent on the first $10 million and three-eighths of a percent on additional sales. Expenses would come out of his commission.

The novel part of Cooke's plan was his projected clientele. Bond issues heretofore had been purchased almost entirely by banks and in large quantities. Cooke proposed to market the bonds to the American people—to convert bond sales from a wholesale business to a retail one. In doing so he would tap into an entirely new stream of investment, and at the same time solve a problem that had vexed previous issues. Banks that purchased bonds typically resold them, and in the process ate into the demand for subsequent issues. Cooke guessed that small purchasers would hold on to their bonds, allowing him to keep selling long past the time previous issues had begun to fail.

Creating a retail market for bonds was no minor task. Cooke began by enlisting local agents. In the larger cities these were often banks and bankers, but in the towns and rural regions they might be anyone with money sense, ambition, and a flair for selling. The agents (and their sub-agents) traveled constantly, drumming up business for bonds the way itinerant peddlers had been drumming for pots, patent medicines, and Bibles for generations. Some wrote their own notices and ad copy; most simply forwarded what Cooke himself composed. "TO FARMERS, MECHANICS AND CAPITALISTS!" read one poster. "You have a solemn duty to perform to your government and posterity! Our gallant army and navy must be supported by every man and woman who has any means, large or small, at their control. The United States Government, to which we owe our prosperity as a nation, security of person and property of every sort, calls on each individual to rally to its support—*not* with donations or gifts—though who could withhold them?—BUT WITH SUBSCRIPTIONS TO HER LOANS."

The appeal to patriotism loosened many purse strings, but actually getting the money out of those purses required educating a whole population in the intricacies of investment. Cooke devised a formula marketers would emulate for generations: the straight man asking questions real customers had but couldn't articulate. Cooke wrote a letter, ostensibly from a farmer in Berks County, Pennsylvania, who intimated he'd buy the bonds assuming he received satisfactory answers to several queries.

1st. Why are they called "Five-Twenties"?

2nd. Do you take country money, or only legal tender? . . .

3rd. Do you sell the Bonds at par?

4th. As I cannot come to Philadelphia, how am I to get the bonds?

5th. What interest do they pay? . . . Is it paid in Gold or legal tenders?

6th. How does Secretary Chase get enough gold to pay this interest?

7th. Will the face of the bond be paid in gold when due?

8th. Can I have the bonds payable to bearer with coupons, or registered and payable to my order?

9th. What sizes are the bonds?

10th. Will I have to pay the same tax on them as I now pay on my railroad or other bonds? . . .

I have no doubt that a good many of my neighbors would like

to take these bonds, and if you will answer my questions I
will show the letter to them.

Cooke, writing now over his own name, answered the questions
one by one.

1st. These Bonds are called "Five-Twenties" because, while
they are *twenty* year bonds they *may* be redeemed by the
Government in GOLD at any time after *five* years. . . .

2nd. Legal tender notes . . . are what the Secretary allows me
to receive. . . .

3rd. The Bonds are sold at PAR, the interest to commence the
day you pay the money.

4th. I have made arrangements with your nearest bank or
banker, who will generally have the Bonds on hand. If not,
you can send the money to me by Express, and I will send
back the Bonds free of cost.

5th. The Bonds pay Six per cent interest in GOLD, *three* per
cent every six months, on the first day of May and
November. . . .

6th. The duties on imports of all articles from abroad must be
paid in GOLD, and this is the way Secretary Chase gets his
gold.

7th. Congress has provided that the Bonds shall be PAID IN
GOLD when due.

8th. You can have either Coupon Bonds payable to the bearer,
or Registered Bonds payable to your order.

9th. The former are in 50's, 100's, 500's, and 1000's; the latter
in the same amounts, also $5000 and $10,000.

10th. No! You will not have to pay any taxes on these Bonds if your income from them does not exceed $600; and on all above $600 you will only have to pay one-half as much income tax as if your money was invested in mortgages or other securities.

Cooke's Berks County farmer became famous as the letter and reply were printed and reprinted in newspapers, magazines, handbills, and broadsides and circulated in every state and territory of the Union. Cooke himself and his agents paid for advertising in papers; in exchange for the ad business, the papers were expected to print articles publicizing the activities of the agents. Few editors felt much conflict of interest, for the bond sales were eminently newsworthy, being the first of their kind in American history. An article from the *Philadelphia Inquirer,* entitled "A Day at the Agency for the Five-Twenty Loan," typified the coverage.

It would rejoice the heart of every patriot if he could witness in person the daily operations at the agency of the national loan in this city. The people are there to give aid and comfort to the government by investing their savings and their capital in the Five-Twenty bonds. They are giving lively exercise to the agent and his clerks, bookkeepers and cashiers. . . . There they sit amidst piles of orders by mail, flights of orders by telegraph, and incessant orders by word of mouth. . . . Here is a letter from a lady in Camden who orders $300. . . . There is one from St. Paul, Minn., for $12,500. Here lies one from Pottsville, Pa., for $1,000, and another from Pittsburgh for

$75,000. Along comes a telegram from Norristown for $250 and close upon the messenger's heels comes another with a dispatch from New York for $250,000. Near one of the desks is a nursery maid who wants a bond for $50, and just behind her, placidly waiting his turn, is a portly gentleman, at whom you can scarcely look without having visions of plethoric pocketbooks and heavy balances in bank. He wants $25,000.

The impression Cooke intended to convey was that everyone was buying the five-twenty bonds. This impression wasn't too far wrong. The bonds went out the door so fast the engravers and printers at the Treasury couldn't keep up. New men were hired and new presses purchased. The register of the Treasury, the person who had to sign all the bonds, nearly paralyzed his arm from overuse. "Poor fellow! I don't see how he stands it," Henry Cooke commiserated. Success fed success. Cooke announced daily sales totals, and papers printed the names of subscribers. In the spring of 1863 the selling became a frenzy. An April day set a record: nearly $2.5 million sold between morning and evening. A week later that record was shattered when five thousand purchasers bought $5 million in a single day.

BY THEN JAY Cooke may have become the person most vital to the Union war effort, after Lincoln. The money Cooke raised kept the Union armies in the field, kept the Europeans—who had widely expected secession to succeed, and generally hoped it would—from recognizing Southern independence, and kept Congress from having to resort to additional legal tender.

Perhaps unsurprisingly, Cooke began acting as though he felt as important as he was. He met periodically with the president; on at least one occasion he counseled Lincoln to change commanders. His excuse for offering military advice was that General George McClellan's reluctance to engage the enemy was preventing bonds from selling as swiftly as they might have otherwise. "Mr. Lincoln had his youngest son on his lap while we were talking," Cooke remembered. "I began by reminding him that the sole charge of raising the vast sums daily required was committed to me, that I was not a politician, that I desired no office, but under God was trying to do my duty in aid of my country, and that now I came to him to plead for a change of commanders of the army, and a more active pressing effort to bring the war to a speedy close. I told him that I came direct from the people, and knew their thoughts." As it happened, Lincoln did replace McClellan not long after this meeting. "So that I have always thought my interview and appeal were the immediate cause of Mr. Lincoln's prompt action," Cooke said.

Cooke exaggerated his influence in this case; regiments of critics had been urging Lincoln to sack McClellan for months. But in another area of policy Cooke's influence was undeniable. Since Andrew Jackson had killed Nicholas Biddle's Bank of the United States, the country had made do with state banks, of which there were some sixteen hundred at the beginning of the Civil War. A system of subtreasuries—the branch offices of the Treasury in various cities—established under James Polk alleviated some of the inconvenience to the federal government of not having a national bank, but by no means all. Cooke, who had grown up with state banks, fully appreciated their deficiencies. "Notes were printed upon every variety of paper, and no two banks issued bills of similar appearance," he said. "It was generally the case that bank notes current in one state could not be circulated in the other states. . . . The banks were breaking constantly, and in many instances circulating notes became almost worthless. Fifty millions of dollars per annum, it is safe to say, would not cover the loss to the people in this country growing out of broken banks, counterfeits, altered notes, and cost of exchange between different points."

Until the Civil War, the inconvenience wasn't so great as to cause Congress to overrule the democratic distrust of the money men. But the war changed that, as it changed so much else. Efficiency claimed priority, and after Congress created a national currency and a national tax code, it began to consider a national banking system. The new national banks would operate under federal charters, like the first and second Banks of the United States, but unlike those institutions they would not be monopolies. Any banks that met certain requirements could receive the federal charters. Of these requirements the most important mandated that a third of a bank's capital take the form of federal bonds, and that its issue of bank notes not exceed ninety percent of the value of the bonds. The nation would benefit from the convenience and reliability of banks operating across several states under uniform charters; the federal government would benefit from the sale of the bonds the banks required.

Opponents of the national banking system—starting with the state bankers and their friends, but including various remnant Jacksonians—raised the obvious constitutional objections. Yet secession and the war had fairly shredded the states' rights arguments, leaving only Hamiltonian nationalists in the field. "There can be no stronger argument in its favor," the *New York Tribune* said of the proposed system, "than that it tends to strengthen the Union by closely interwoven ties of common interest in the permanence and credit of the National Government."

Jay Cooke initially had reservations, not wishing to antagonize the state bankers who were acting as his bond agents. But when Chase made clear that he would have his national banking system with Cooke or without him, Cooke reconsidered. "Seeing that he was so earnest in the matter, I obtained from him a copy of his bill, and my brother Henry and I sat up until midnight reading it over and discussing it. It was a very voluminous bill and required a good deal of pruning. Next morning we went to Mr. Chase and told him that we had decided to take up the matter and endeavor to pass the measure."

Cooke strong-armed the newspapers he was patronizing. "We felt that we had a right to claim their columns, in which to set forth the merits of the new national banking system. I suggested the substance of editorials, some of which I wrote, but they were mostly written by my brother"—former editor Henry. For six weeks the Cooke brothers flooded the newsrooms with copy, adducing reasons weighty and slight for passage of Chase's bill. They then purchased copies of the papers that printed the articles and laid them on the desks of wavering legislators, with each member getting the papers from his state or district, showing the groundswell of support for the national system. The result was a stunning triumph. "At first the banking project was pronounced a scheme of Mr. Chase that would be ridiculed out of Congress," the *Philadelphia Press* explained. "It was compared to the Utopian money plans of other days. . . . In a comparatively short space of time these objections have been refuted to the satisfaction of a large majority of the people, and many who were first and most earnest in resisting the measure are now giving it their warm support." That this article, too, might have been bought by Cooke didn't diminish the truth of its argument. The banking bill passed the Senate by two votes and the House by fourteen; on February 25, 1863, Lincoln gave it his signature.

COOKE NOT UNREASONABLY expected gratitude from Chase for his campaign on behalf of the banking bill. And he did receive the new law's initial charter, for the First National Bank of Philadelphia. But before long a noticeable cooling occurred between the secretary and the bond master. Chase had never lost his ambition for the presidency, and as the war entered its fourth year he thought Lincoln was vulnerable. Yet he needed to counter criticism that he was too cozy with the money men, especially Jay Cooke. So he picked fights with Cooke—over the expenses of the bond campaign and over the commissions Cooke and his agents were paid. Chase unilaterally reduced Cooke's commission on the five-twenty sale from the original three-eighths percent past $10 million to one-quarter, and he penalized Cooke for overselling his quota by refusing to pay any commission for sales beyond the $500 million originally authorized (sales totaled nearly $511 million).

Cooke felt wronged. "I have constantly risked my whole fortune . . . have made expenditures of money prior to any sales of bonds . . . have increased three-fold the expenses of my different offices . . . have struggled through the year with a weight of care and anxiety upon me," he complained to Chase. He offered to forgo future compensation entirely if the Treasury would assume expenses and risk.

But he knew his recourse was limited. He couldn't well sue, for the administration made a practice of ignoring judicial rulings that went against it. Neither could he expect sympathy from Congress, whose members found it convenient to blame him—a more tempting target than either Lincoln or themselves—for the high cost of the war. In fact, when Congress authorized a new bond issue, it explicitly barred any single person from exercising the control of sales Cooke had wielded over the five-twenties.

The setback was temporary. Chase's presidential efforts imploded and he was forced from the Treasury, and the new bond issues languished in the absence of the Cooke marketing magic. Cooke wasn't surprised when the new Treasury secretary, William Fessenden, turned to him and asked him to move the new bonds.

Yet the invitation wasn't quite irresistible. "Some passages of this letter are more fit for the instructions to a fool or a dishonest agent than one deserving confidence and tried and trusted heretofore to millions," Cooke wrote to Henry regarding Fessenden's proffered terms. "I am not disposed to work my life blood out under such depressing circumstances."

Fortunately for the Union war effort, Fessenden followed Chase out the Treasury door. He was succeeded by Hugh McCulloch, who, unlike both Chase and Fessenden, actually knew something about banking. He and Cooke came to terms, and Cooke began selling "seven-thirties"—named this time for the interest rate: 7.30 percent—with the same infectious gusto he had employed to market the five-twenties. A visitor to the Philadelphia office described him in his element.

> He is a large man who gives you instantly the impression of not having done growing—of having a great deal of youth straggling behind his manhood, and that has not yet marched up but is going to come in soon and camp right down on the table at which he is writing. You don't see 7-30s in him at your first look . . . nor any finance, nor any statesmanship, nor any power. But you do see . . . the boyish freshness of his face, the boyish weight and disorder of his brown hair, the childlike brightness of eyes behind whose laughter you see thinking going on, the superabounding suppleness and quickness of full-muscled boyhood in a large man's motion. Certainly that man shall quit banking soon and play leap frog. You are sure of it.

The seven-thirty bonds sold even faster than the five-twenties had. Within six months Cooke brought in $830 million for the Union government. The seven-thirty sale was all the more astonishing on account of the huge sales that had preceded it, and the fact that the war ended before the bond drive was half finished. But Appomattox merely prompted Cooke to soft-pedal the patriotism in his sales pitch and emphasize financial self-interest. So successfully did Cooke negotiate the transition from war to peace that the Union bonds found buyers, after the Confederate surrender, even in parts of the South.

The triumph of the seven-thirty campaign, in the afterglow of the Union victory, made Cooke America's first celebrity banker. "The fame of Jay Cooke is now world-wide," one newspaper informed its readers. Another declared, "This nation owes a debt of gratitude to Jay Cooke that it cannot soon discharge. Without his valuable aid the wheels of government might frequently have

A promotional poster for Jay Cooke's "7-30" campaign. This appeal, a variant of his famous letter to the Berks County farmer, summarizes Cooke's case for purchasing Union debt: "Nothing can be safer, for we are all bound for it."

been seriously entangled." Still another captured the secret of Cooke's success when it said, "The greatest banking firm in the world is that of Jay Cooke and the American people—the latter being the true 'Company' of the firm. The Rothschilds, the Barings, the Hopes are mere curbstone brokers in comparison." This paper proposed to turn the entire government over to Cooke. "We think the whole business of all the departments might be done for an eighth of one per cent."

This last reference was to Cooke's profit on the latest bond sales, and it approximated his net on the sales overall. Cooke & Company sold considerably more than a billion dollars in bonds during and just after the war (or more than twenty times what the associated bankers at the beginning of the war had considered sufficient) and realized, after expenses, about $1.7 million. This was more than pocket change, but considering that bond sales before Cooke had often involved commissions and fees of five percent or more, Cooke's operation was breathtakingly efficient. It was no wonder his fellow bankers despised him, for revealing the lard in their money game. Nor was it remarkable that a Confederate leader declared, in grudging admiration of Cooke's accomplishment, "The Yankees did not whip us in the field. We were whipped in the Treasury Department."

4

The Great Gold Conspiracy

The Civil War began as a revolt by Southern democrats
and ended as a revolution by Northern capitalists. The
secessionists were the small-government, states'-rights
heirs of Jefferson; the anti-secessionists were the big-govern-
ment, nationalist descendants of Hamilton. Slavery had blurred
the distinction somewhat: the Georgia planter with five hundred
slaves was rather less the exemplar of equality on which democracy prided itself than the Iowa farmer with his half-section. But
slavery had always blurred the distinction; Jefferson himself
owned two hundred slaves. On the matter of the role of government and its relation to capital, the lines were clearer—and they
grew clearer still as the Civil War progressed. The planters lost
their slaves; the capitalists won control of the national government. The capitalists created a national currency, a national tax
code, a national banking system, and a national system of credit;
on the side they steepened tariffs to protect the national market
and commenced construction of a nationally funded railway to

the Pacific. At war's end there was little the capitalists could ask of government they hadn't already received. Democracy didn't exactly lose the war, as the millions of freedmen could attest. But capitalism plainly won.

Put otherwise, just as the war emancipated the slaves, so it emancipated the capitalists. The shackles of slavery had bound the capitalists too, as Southern senators wielded a veto over the projects the capitalists had long desired. Secession suspended the veto, leaving the party of capitalism in control of the federal government. And the Southern defeat broke the power of the slaveholders in the South itself, opening that region to capitalist penetration. In 1865 the capitalists could look out across America and see nothing but opportunity.

THE GREATEST OPPORTUNITIES were closest to home. The war completed the consolidation of New York City's position as the country's financial capital. In the eighteenth century Philadelphia had held first place in the hearts of the money men. But that primacy had begun to weaken when Hamilton cut his deal regarding the debt and sent the seat of government south. The opening of the Erie Canal in 1825 made New York the commercial entrepôt to the interior, giving bankers and brokers reason to headquarter on the Hudson. Jackson's defeat of Biddle, and the ignominious collapse of the remnant Bank of the United States, further weakened the Pennsylvania city, even as the rise of railroads, anchored in the East at New York, entrenched New York's commercial advantage. The growing alienation of the

South gave the money men a final reason for looking and moving farther north.

The move from Philadelphia involved some innovation. The nineteenth century in America saw the emergence of stock exchanges where the shares of corporations were bought and sold. Entrepreneurs had long entered into partnerships to pool resources and spread risk, but as America began to industrialize, the partnerships became larger and more common. Brokers initially gathered informally to buy and sell shares; the most important such gathering dated from 1792, when a band of traders had met under a buttonwood, or sycamore, tree at what would become 68 Wall Street in lower Manhattan, not far from the local branch of Alexander Hamilton's Bank of the United States. The Buttonwood Agreement pledged the signatories to observe certain standards in the buying and selling of shares. For the next two decades the New York stock market remained an outdoor affair, but by the time the buttonwood tree went the way of all urban timber the traders had moved indoors and were calling themselves the New York Stock and Exchange Board (later simply the New York Stock Exchange). Similar exchanges sprang up in other cities, although none matched New York's for the volume and diversity of stocks traded.

During the 1850s and 1860s the most active trading took place in the shares of railroad corporations. The birth and growth of railroads required a transformation in capitalist thinking. Where previous companies had employed tens or perhaps hundreds of workers, railroads employed thousands and eventually tens of thousands. Where older companies operated in one city

RR
more
offices
less
expensive

or at most a few, railroads had offices and depots in dozens or scores of cities and towns scattered across entire states and regions. Where earlier enterprises had needed tens or hundreds of thousands of dollars to commence or expand operations, rail-roads required tens or hundreds of millions of dollars.

This last requirement was what engaged the money men, who sold the shares in exchange for the capital that enabled the rail-roads to build and grow. Initial offerings got the railroads started; if the railroads prospered, the shares increased in value, enticing new investors but also speculators, whose interest lay less in the long-term strength of the roads than in the short-term perform-ance of their share prices. Because railroads were novel, and because trading on this scale was unprecedented, few rules con-strained the speculators. The single sure guide was caveat emptor.

Speculators required a rare combination of analytical clever-ness and marketing brass. When these didn't appear in a single person, collaborations developed, as among Jay Gould, Daniel Drew, and Jim Fisk. No cleverer analyst of American stocks ever lived than Gould. As a boy in upstate New York he showed an aptitude for mathematics, convincing his farmer father he was destined for other things than the plow. He learned to survey, converting hills and dales to maps and numbers. He also learned to spot economic opportunities. After discovering that the hem-lock trees among which he had been surveying were used to tan hides, he opened a tannery. The business didn't particularly pros-per, not least because Gould's partner committed suicide, but the experience awakened in Gould a desire for greater success and a passion for the details of finance. "When intensely interested in any matter," an associate later said of Gould, "he devoted his whole concentration of thought upon that one thing, and would seem to lose interest in things often of greater pecuniary importance but of not so much commercial fascination. He loved the intricacies and perplexities of financial problems."

With many another ambitious upstater, Gould followed the Hudson down to the land of opportunity at its mouth. He arrived in time for the Civil War, which besides placing the party of capitalism in command of American politics created unusual opportunities for speculation. Daniel Drew, who introduced Gould to the speculative arts, explained, "Along with the ordinary happenings, we fellows in Wall Street had the fortunes of war to speculate about. . . . That always makes great doings on a stock exchange. It's good fishing in troubled waters."

Gould angled especially in railroad stocks. The big fish of the market was the Erie Railroad, which linked New York City to Buffalo and beyond, and whose corporate fortunes had tempted investors for years. The old man of the sea in which the Erie swam was Cornelius Vanderbilt, the richest person in America and a capitalist known for bare-knuckled bruising. Vanderbilt was past his physical prime; he no longer literally beat his corporate rivals. But he did so metaphorically, and he was determined to take the Erie.

Yet the Commodore, as Vanderbilt had been called since his time as a steamship magnate, was the product of an earlier stage of capitalism. He was a cutthroat when it came to prices on his watercraft and a briber of judges and elected officials, but pure speculation—the black art of driving shares up and down for the

joy and profit of the game—wasn't his forte. And in the fight for
the Erie Railroad he was outnumbered besides. Jay Gould joined
forces with Drew, the reigning virtuoso of railroad speculation.
"Uncle Dan" had come to corporate stock from live stock; as a
drover who trailed his beeves to Manhattan he pioneered fina-
gles that long survived him and added phrases to the Wall Street
lexicon. Drew became notorious for "watering stock"—salting
the feed of his cattle so they would gain weight before sale—and
for adapting the technique to corporate shares. His dalliance
with the Erie earned that company a reputation as the "scarlet
woman of Wall Street." Other speculators openly admired his
work. "Daniel says up, Erie goes up," a brokers' proverb asserted.
"Daniel says down, Erie goes down. Daniel says wiggle-waggle,
Erie bobs both ways."

To make a trio, Gould and Drew enlisted James Fisk Jr. Fisk
came to New York from Vermont, where his father had raised
him to be a peddler. Young Jim learned early that peddlers who
caused a commotion did better than their inconspicuous colleagues; by the time he was twenty he'd decked out his peddling
carts like a circus caravan and made his arrival the most anticipated event of any New England season. In time he found his
way to New York, where Drew took him under his wing—and
relieved him of every dollar he owned. A lesser man might have
been put off by the swindle, but Fisk concluded that anyone so
deft deserved serious study.

Gradually and, at first, quietly the threesome of Gould, Drew,
and Fisk bought shares of the Erie with mostly borrowed money.
They intended to gain control, strip the road of its salable assets,

and dump the carcass back on the market. They might have done so without incident had they not crossed the path of Vanderbilt, who took offense at the Erie's activities east of Chicago, where one of his lines already dominated the market. Vanderbilt reached far into his deep pockets to purchase sufficient Erie stock to preempt the Gould group and gain control for himself.

domestic competition

The New York papers labeled the ensuing contest the "Erie War," and they reported every sally, attack, and counteroffensive in gory detail. Rumors and planted news stories constituted the small-arms fire, the purchase of judges and injunctions the heavier shelling. The Gould cabal manipulated proxies to seize control of the Erie's executive committee, and they answered Vanderbilt's bloc purchases of shares with the issue of new blocs. "If this printing press don't break down," Fisk declared, "I'll be damned if I don't give the old hog all he wants of Erie."

= "The Erie War"

The climax came when Vanderbilt got a judge to enjoin any further issues and sent the police to enforce the order against the Gould trio and their minions. "Their only chance of escape from incarceration lay in precipitate flight," reported Charles Francis Adams Jr., the author of the soberest contemporary account of the affair.

> The astonished police saw a throng of panic-stricken railway directors, looking more like a frightened gang of thieves, disturbed in the division of their plunder, than like the wealthy representatives of a great corporation, rush headlong from the doors of the Erie office and dash off in the direction of the Jersey ferry. In their hands were packages and files of papers,

and their pockets were crammed with assets and securities. One individual bore away with him in a hackney coach bales containing six millions of dollars in greenbacks. Other members of the board followed under cover of the night; some of them, not daring to expose themselves to the publicity of a ferry, attempted to cross in open boats concealed by darkness and a March fog.

In New Jersey the conspirators were safe, as the courts of that commonwealth didn't extradite persons accused of such minor peccadilloes as business fraud. This tolerance wasn't so much a moral commentary as a competitive practice: New Jersey hoped to entice corporations to charter in the Garden State, as the Erie thereupon did, leaving Vanderbilt apoplectic on the Hudson's eastern shore. Yet to ensure his acquiescence in their coup, Gould and the others paid him a reported $1 million to drop his lawsuits and desist from trying to reclaim the road.

AS EVENTS SOON proved, the Erie War was simply practice for a more ambitious assault by Gould and Fisk. The target this time was no mere corporation but the money supply of the United States. America's money still bore the marks of the suspension of specie payments in 1861 and the issue of greenbacks the following year. Since then the country had operated a dual system: greenbacks for domestic commerce, gold for the payment of customs duties and for international transactions. (Silver had effectively disappeared from circulation during the California gold rush, which made gold relatively cheaper than silver and caused people to hoard the latter.)

The two systems intertwined in the Gold Room, a special section of the New York exchange where speculators and persons with pedestrian need for gold traded the yellow metal for greenbacks. Within weeks of its opening in 1862 the Gold Room developed a reputation as the den of the most dangerous transactions. One regular called it "a cavern full of dank and noisome vapors" where "the deadly carbonic acid was blended with the fumes of stale smoke and vinous breaths." A journalist wrote, "Imagine a rat-pit in full blast, with twenty or thirty men ranged around the rat tragedy, each with a canine under his arm, yelling and howling at once." The center of the room contained a stony Cupid spewing water into the air. "The artistic conception is not appropriate," the journalist complained. "Instead of a Cupid throwing a pearly fountain into the air, there should have been a hungry Midas turning everything to gold and starving from sheer inability to eat."

As during the Civil War, the greater value of gold compared to paper resulted in a postwar premium for the former, which during 1868 and early 1869 ranged from about 35 to 42 (meaning that 135 to 142 paper dollars were required to purchase 100 gold dollars). The variation in prices tempted speculators to bet on their direction. "Bulls" took "long" positions in gold—they purchased gold and hoped for a rise in price, after which they would sell and pocket the profit. "Bears" took "short" positions—sold gold they had borrowed, anticipating a price fall before they had to buy the gold back to repay their lenders. The bears, or shorts, were generally thought to be in the more precarious position, for if the price *rose* between the short sale and the required repayment, they had to swallow the loss or renege on their contracts. Put differently, the largest loss a long buyer could suffer was the amount of the purchase price (since the price of gold, like that of other commodities, couldn't fall below zero), while a short seller could lose an unlimited amount (there being no upper limit on prices).

In this regard gold was no different from any other stock or commodity. But in another sense gold was very different. Gyrations in the price of pork bellies or Erie shares affected adjacent sectors of the economy but rarely threatened the financial system as a whole. By contrast, gyrations in gold—which were nothing more or less than surges and plunges in the value of the dollar—discombobulated the entire economy. For this reason the federal government treated the gold market differently than it treated the market in shares and commodities. The government held a reserve supply of gold. If the gold price rose abruptly, the government might sell gold and drive the price down. If the gold price dropped, it could buy gold and pull the price back up.

Various parties preferred different price levels for gold. Importers liked low prices, partly because the low prices eased the burden of paying their import duties, but mostly because cheap gold corresponded to a strong dollar, making imports less expensive. Conversely, exporters desired high prices for gold, which meant a cheap dollar and a larger foreign market for the goods they shipped abroad. The speculators—the bulls and bears—cared less about the absolute price of gold than about changes in price.

Jay Gould's interests in gold combined those of the exporter and of the speculator. Gould wasn't an exporter himself, but many of the customers of his Erie Railroad were, and when demand for their products—typically grain—increased, so did the traffic on the railroad. This export interest, he said, was what attracted his attention to the gold price during the spring and summer of 1869. "Business got very dull after the inauguration," he told a congressional committee, referring to the inauguration of Ulysses Grant. "Gold went down to about 30 and stopped the movement of produce. Our business in consequence fell off very much. . . . I had a careful examination made, and I found that with gold at 40 or 45, Americans would supply the English market with breadstuffs, but that it would require gold to be at that price to equalize our high-priced labor and our rail transportation with the low-priced labor and the water transportation from the Mediterranean. With gold below 40 we could not export, but with gold above 45 we would get the trade."

Though the committee questioning Gould had charge of banking and commerce, the exchange-rate theories that underlay greenback-gold conversions and connected them to foreign trade were sufficiently new that the members insisted that Gould elaborate. "How will the rise in gold give American produce the foreign market?" chairman James Garfield, a Republican of Ohio, asked.

"The farmers of the West are pretty rich," Gould replied. "And they sell very reluctantly unless they get a profit upon their products. Labor and rail transportation are high, and rather than do business at a loss they will let their produce lie. But as the price of gold goes up the price of wheat goes up. Last spring, when the

Secretary"—of the Treasury, Hugh McCulloch—"sold gold, we had in one day orders stopped for 400 cars that were ordered to ship grain. The sale of gold fell like a pall upon the country."

Gould explained that he hoped to lift the pall by pushing up the price of gold. "I bought gold along in the spring," he told the committee. The bears had been beating down gold—spreading rumors of bad business ahead—and Gould decided he had to act. "I took it at their price, and put it up four or five per cent, which started my business a little, and I sold my gold out." But then the new secretary of the Treasury, George Boutwell, began selling gold. "He went in and threw a large amount on the market, taking in greenbacks for it and making money very stringent. That stopped business the second time, and it got so that we were not doing anything. . . . I went in a second time. That must have been in July or August. At that time the fact was established that we had an immense harvest, and that there was going to be a large surplus of breadstuffs, either to rot or to be exported."

The committee's interest in Gould reflected reports that he had engaged in a speculative conspiracy. Chairman Garfield inquired about Gould's associates in the gold purchases, mentioning two brokers in particular. Gould denied a conspiracy but explained a simple fact of market life. "We bought gold together, and each would take his gold and pay for it. The reason we bought it together was that if two or three parties were in the market buying gold at the same time they would bid it up, but if only one party bid for the whole, he would buy cheap. . . . We bought it together and divided it pro rata." Gould added that the gold market was filled with "a lot of speculators," starting with the brokers who handled gold orders. "When a man goes into the market who they think has some power, they watch him, and if he gives them an order to buy a hundred thousand dollars, they will first buy three or four hundred thousand dollars on their own account." This afforded them the benefit of any price rise, but it also made their client's purchase more expensive. "So, in order to conceal the movement, we would sometimes give an order to sell while we were really buying."

Some committee members must have wondered at this explanation. If Gould's purpose, as he had stated, was to push up the price of gold, he should have been happy for others to know he and his partners were buying. But none of the members pressed him on it, and the questioning turned to attempts Gould might

Jay Gould, who grew the beard to make himself appear older and more responsible. Many investors were taken in.

have made to influence public policy. He answered carefully but tantalizingly. "I supposed it was the policy of the administration to let gold work up until after the fall crops were moved. And I had good reason to suppose that was to be so, or I should never have gone into this movement." Garfield pressed him to explain further. Gould responded that he had received a visit from Abel Corbin, the new husband of President Grant's sister. Gould had known Corbin casually for some time. "He came to see me, wanted to make some money, and asked my opinion." Garfield asked Gould who had initiated the meeting. Gould's memory failed. "It does not occur to me at this moment whether I sought him or he sought me. I used to meet him occasionally." Gould at once realized this sounded evasive, especially since he had declared, only moments before, that his memory had always sufficed to let him dispense with ledgers and other accounts in recording his business. "I carried the whole thing in my head. . . . I never kept a book in my life." So now he expanded on his relationship with Corbin, whom he described as "a very shrewd old gentleman, much more far-seeing than the newspapers give him credit for." Gould said he had told Corbin of his theory of gold prices and exports. "He saw at a glance the whole case, and said that he thought it was the true platform to stand on; that whatever the government could do legitimately and fairly to facilitate the exportation of breadstuffs and produce good prices for the products of the West, they ought to do. He was anxious that I should see the President." Corbin arranged a meeting between Grant and Gould at his own house on a day when Grant was visiting.

This first meeting was uneventful, but it led to another, in June aboard one of the packet boats operated by the Erie between New York and Boston. The president was traveling north to attend a peace jubilee commemorating the victory in the Civil War, and Gould, Fisk, and some others joined him en route. "He was our guest," Gould explained. "We had supper about nine or ten o'clock. . . . At this supper the question came up about the state of the country, the crops, the prospects ahead, et cetera. The President was a listener; the other gentlemen were discussing." Fisk, when questioned by the committee separately, offered a different version of the president's participation. "He entered into the conversation with a good deal of spirit," Fisk said. But Gould and Fisk agreed that Grant gave them no encouragement. "He remarked that he thought there was a certain amount of fictitiousness about the prosperity of the country," Gould said, "and that the bubble might as well be tapped in one way as another." Grant then asked Gould's opinion. "I remarked that I thought if that policy was carried out, it would produce great distress, and almost lead to civil war; it would produce strikes among the workmen, and the workshops, to a great extent, would have to be closed. The manufactories would have to stop. I took the ground that the government ought to let gold alone, and let it find its commercial level—that, as a matter of fact, it ought to facilitate an upward movement of gold in the fall." The president was not convinced. "The interview . . . was a wet blanket," Gould declared. "We supposed from that conversation that the President was a contractionist." Fisk drew the same conclusion. "When we got to Boston . . . the prospect did not look promising," he said.

A less resourceful person than Gould might have abandoned

his cause at this point. The president could break the market for gold at any moment simply by ordering the Treasury to sell. Yet Gould decided to play for time, hoping the president would come around. In August he planted an un-bylined story in the *New York Times* intimating inside knowledge of the administration's financial plans and declaring, "At a time of the year so critical to producers, the President will not withdraw currency from the channels of trade and commerce; he will not send gold into the market and sell it for currency." Gould got Corbin to arrange another meeting with Grant, which proved far more encouraging than the earlier session. "The President had changed his views," Gould recounted. "He was satisfied that the country had a very bountiful harvest; that there was to be a large surplus; that unless we could find a large market abroad for that surplus it would put down prices here. . . . He remarked that the government would do nothing during the fall months of the year to put down the price of gold or make money tight. On the contrary, they would do everything they could to facilitate the movement of bread-stuffs. He seemed to take a very deep interest in it; it seemed to have been a matter of study with him."

Encouraged, Gould pressed forward. He secured Corbin's continued cooperation by purchasing $1.5 million of gold for his account, with the consequence for Corbin that every point's rise in the gold price put more than $10,000 in his pocket. Corbin helped him arrange the appointment of Daniel Butterfield to be assistant Treasury secretary for New York, with oversight of gold sales. Gould apparently purchased gold for Butterfield too, although Butterfield later denied it.

One might have expected Gould to keep these arrangements secret lest word get out that he was trying to bribe the government. In fact he did just the opposite, feeding the news to the rumormongers of Wall Street. Gould didn't know whether he could count on the support of Corbin and Butterfield, but he wanted the world to think he could, that he had connections high inside the administration. He apparently started a story that his influence reached into the Executive Mansion itself. Mrs. Grant was said to have a gold account with Gould. No records ever surfaced that showed she did, but Fisk testified that Corbin had told him directly "that Mrs. Grant had an interest . . . that Mr. Corbin held for himself about two millions of gold, five hundred thousand of which was for Mrs. Grant."

As the rumors churned, Gould bought gold. His immediate purpose was what he had said all along: to depress the dollar enough to get the crops moving and keep his rail cars full. But a second objective gradually emerged: to corner the gold market. Corners come in shades and flavors, but at the heart of any corner is a plot by a single person or coalition to gain control of enough of a stock or commodity to prevent fulfillment of obligations in that item. Short sellers in the stock or commodity have to buy it to meet their commitments; if the cornerer controls so much that the short sellers can't find what they need, the cornerer can dictate price or terms of settlement. As Gould bought more and more gold, he realized he might be able to corner the yellow metal, which would be the coup of any speculator's lifetime.

Gould never admitted to any such plan. "I did not want to buy

so much gold," he told the congressional investigators. "I never
intended to purchase more than four or five millions of gold. . . .
I had no idea of cornering it." He said he simply hoped to push
gold up long enough to move the harvest. Then he would sell,
with luck while gold was still high, and let it fall back to its previous level. "My theory was that if gold could stay at 40 or 45 till
after the 1st of January, we could export about a hundred millions of produce, and that would turn the current of exchange in
our favor. . . . Gold would flow in here from Paris and London,
and that would create a downward tendency in gold, and it would
fall just as a ripe apple." By then he would be out of gold and into
something else.

But the gold bears got in the way, he said. "These fellows went
in and sold short, so that in order to keep it up, I had to buy or
else back down and show the white feather."

PERHAPS GOULD WAS telling the truth. Perhaps the gold corner wasn't his initial idea—although the secrecy surrounding his
early purchases suggests more than an effort to boost gold prices.
But the longer his position in gold grew, the more feasible a corner
appeared and, for that reason, the more attractive. He laid his
plans carefully. He cozied up to Daniel Butterfield, who didn't
determine Treasury policy but could alert Gould to any policy
change. The greatest threat to Gould's scheme was a decision by
the administration to sell gold. That decision would be transmit-
ted to Butterfield in New York, who could tip Gould in advance
and allow him to get out of the market before his rivals did.

To keep the administration from selling, Gould approached the president again, this time obliquely. In mid-September he had Corbin write a letter to Grant, who was vacationing in western Pennsylvania. The letter, without revealing Corbin's personal interest in the matter, urged the president to let the market determine the price of gold. Gould asked Fisk, who had begun buying gold, too, to arrange for a special courier to deliver Corbin's letter. The courier, W. O. Chapin, rode a train to Pittsburgh and then hired a carriage for the final thirty miles to Grant's vacation residence. He arrived while Grant was playing croquet with Horace Porter, his private secretary. "I was told that there was a gentleman there who wanted to see me," Porter testified. "I sent him word to wait till we had finished the game." A few minutes later Porter and Grant came up to the house, with the president taking a seat on the porch and Porter going inside to meet Chapin. Chapin carried a letter from Corbin to Porter, introducing Chapin and explaining that he had a message to deliver to the president. Porter asked Grant to enter the parlor. Chapin produced the letter from Corbin to Grant, which the president read carefully. Chapin asked if there was any reply. Grant said there was none.

Chapin had instructions from Fisk to telegraph him upon completion of the assignment. Chapin hurried to the nearest telegraph office and sent a message: "LETTERS DELIVERED ALL RIGHT." Fisk apparently parsed the reply differently than Chapin intended, concluding that "all right" constituted Grant's response to Corbin's plea to keep the government out of the market. On this premise he and Gould continued their gold purchases.

But Gould soon discovered that all was not right. Grant realized only after Chapin left that he wasn't the ordinary postal delivery clerk, and as he began to wonder why Corbin would go to the trouble of sending a man clear from New York, he pieced together Corbin's involvement in the gold affair. Mrs. Grant happened to be writing to Mrs. Corbin a short while later, and Grant suggested that she tell her sister that rumors were linking her husband to gold speculators in New York, and that these rumors were greatly distressing the president.

Julia Grant's letter reached Virginia Corbin the following day. She shared the message with her husband, who went to Gould in alarm. Corbin said he had to get out of the market at once. "He figured up that his gold, at the price it then stood, if sold would give him about $150,000 profit, and he wanted me to take the gold off his hands," Gould recounted. Gould resisted, urging Corbin to be brave. He said that he'd guarantee Corbin's current profit, but that to throw the gold on the market just then would give the plan away. And Corbin must keep absolutely quiet about the letter from Julia Grant. "I am undone if that letter gets out," he told Corbin.

What Gould didn't tell Corbin was that he was nearly undone already. Grant knew something shady was going on, and he certainly wouldn't tolerate a gold corner, which would throw the country's entire financial structure into turmoil. The only question was when Grant would give the order to dump the Treasury gold onto the market.

Realizing the corner was now impossible, Gould pondered how to extricate himself. So far only he and Corbin knew what

Grant knew. Corbin had no reason to share the intelligence. And Gould saw no reason to share it, either, not even with Fisk. Though the two men were partners, they didn't do everything together. In the gold project they apparently kept separate accounts, acting more as allies than partners. Gould decided that the only way to save himself was to sacrifice Fisk—to let Fisk continue to think everything was all right. Perhaps Gould reasoned that if he himself survived the debacle that was increasingly inevitable, he could make it up to Fisk in the future.

Gould began selling—slowly, stealthily, covering his tracks with small purchases to give the impression he was still a buyer—even as he let Fisk drive the price upward. Fisk relished his role as the leading bull and played the part to perfection. During the fourth week of September he drove gold higher and higher. On Thursday, September 23, he rode from the opera house he and Gould had converted into offices for the Erie to the Gold Room, where he taunted the bears and personally urged his brokers to buy at any price. As the price topped 140 he offered to wager it would pass 145 before day's end. The directors of the Gold Room had recently installed an electric indicator that showed the current price; with each tick that the pointer moved upward, the bears suffered the more, while the bulls—including scores of speculators who had jumped on the Gould-Fisk bandwagon—celebrated their mounting good fortune. "The bear party at times seemed to be perfectly frantic while undergoing punishment at the hands of the exultant and defiant bulls," a financial correspondent related. "And as the roar of battle and the screams of the victims resounded through New Street, it seemed as though human nature was undergoing torments worse than any that Dante ever witnessed in hell."

By the close of business Thursday the market was in disarray from the large volume of sales. A typical day's sale was $70 million; that day it reached nearly $240 million. The ledger men lagged hours behind the transactions. Fisk retired to the Opera House to toast his good fortune with Gould, who proved considerably more subdued. In another man, Fisk might have suspected something. But Gould was famous for keeping his own counsel, and he kept it now. "I had my own views about the market, and had my own fish to fry," he remarked afterward. "Very likely I listened to what was said, but it went in one ear and out of the other. I was all alone, so to speak, in what I did, and I did not let any of those people know exactly how I stood."

Fisk and the bulls plotted how to squeeze the bears most painfully. The pool held commitments for delivery of more than $100 million, at a time when barely $15 million in gold and gold certificates circulated in New York outside the vaults of the subtreasury there. Someone suggested publishing the names of the shorts—a group that included more than two hundred of the city's most prominent bankers, brokers, and merchants—and the amounts they owed. The bad publicity alone would bring many to their knees, and they would beg to settle at whatever terms the bulls required. But someone else suggested that such a course might constitute—or indicate—criminal conspiracy. And there was no telling what the desperate bears might do by way of personal injury to particular bulls. The extortion scheme was shelved.

But it scarcely seemed necessary. With the commitments so far ahead of the available supply, the corner seemed assured. The bulls slept the slumber of the confident while the bears prepared their financial wills.

The next morning's papers predicted carnage worse than the day before. The *New York Times* declared a "practical *corner* in gold" and repeated the rumors the bulls had been spreading. "The highest official in the land was quoted *as being with them,* and he, of course, controls the action of the Secretary of the Treasury and the New York assistant treasurer." The *Times* questioned the rumors but observed that their effect had been to produce the widespread conviction that the Grant administration would let the market run its course and would not sell Treasury gold. The consequence was that commodity and exchange markets were "paralyzed by this heavy rise and *corner* in gold, *through a sheer gambling operation.*" The economy verged on ruin. "The government is scandalized . . . the public credit damaged . . . the general trade of the country agitated. . . . When or where the trouble is to end we have no present means of telling."

scandal

Long before the Gold Room opened that Friday morning the bulls began trading on the curb outside; at the ten o'clock bell the gold indicator leaped instantly from 143 to 150. "Take all that you can get," Fisk ordered his brokers. The price lurched upward again, to 155.

The tumult immediately spread to the stock exchange. The gold speculation had sucked funds out of scores of banks, which now teetered on insolvency. Brokers were even more exposed, having fewer resources and comparatively larger speculative accounts. One stockbroker was so maddened he threatened to shoot one of the gold bulls. The bull responded by striding into the stock exchange, tossing off his coat, tearing open his shirt, and daring anyone to fire. When no one did, he returned to the Gold Room and triumphantly resumed his trading.

Gould and Fisk continued to work at cross-purposes, the former selling silently, the latter buying noisily. "Take all you can get at 160," Fisk shouted. The bulls predicted gold would reach 200, and the price continued to climb.

A threat to the bulls developed when bank examiners arrived at the Tenth National Bank, the institution Gould and Fisk had purchased to finance their speculation. As they lacked cash to fund their purchases, they paid with certified checks on the Tenth National. The checks far exceeded the bank's existing ability to pay, but if the speculation succeeded they would be covered before anyone found out. The arrival of the examiners—which may or may not have been mere coincidence—threatened to reveal the sham behind the checks. But whether the examiners were crooked or merely incompetent, they failed to spot the fraud being committed beneath their noses.

From Washington the Grant administration monitored the market closely. Grant had returned from Pennsylvania the previous afternoon, and he called for Treasury secretary Boutwell that evening. Together they read the telegraphed reports from New York and came to a firm conclusion. "If gold advanced materially the next day," Boutwell explained afterward, "it would be our duty to sell." How much Grant told Boutwell regarding his suspicions of conspiracy is unclear. Given that the only conspirator

he knew about at this time was his brother-in-law, he might well
have said nothing. Boutwell remarked later that if the contest
had been simply an ordinary struggle among speculators, the
administration might have kept hands off. Any decision doubt-
less would have been interpreted as favoring one side or the
other. "The President was anxious, as I was, that we should not
interfere unless it seemed to be an absolute necessity." But they
seemed to have no choice. "We thought the business of the
country was in danger. . . . If banking institutions should become
involved and break, we might have a repetition of such disasters
as we had in 1857"—when the *Central America* had sunk and
taken Wall Street with it.

At eleven o'clock Friday morning Boutwell received a rush
telegram from Daniel Butterfield in New York. "Gold over one
hundred and sixty," Butterfield wrote. "Moving up every hour."
Boutwell returned to the White House. "The time had come
when we must interfere," he recalled thinking. Grant agreed.
"He expressed the opinion . . . that we ought to sell $5 million."
Boutwell had judged $3 million sufficient; they split the differ-
ence. Boutwell sent a telegram by Western Union to Butterfield
directing him to announce the sale of $4 million in federal gold.
Then—"apprehending that there might be trouble, or that some
interested party might get possession of it [the Western Union
telegram]"—the secretary sent the same message by a second
line, operated by the Franklin Telegraph Company.

The first telegram left Washington at 11:42, the second at 11:45.
Standard time zones hadn't been invented yet, and in those days
New York was twelve minutes ahead of Washington. Apparently the

Franklin company was more efficient than Western Union, for the message sent by the former reached the New York subtreasury at 12:05 local time, while that sent by the latter didn't arrive until 12:10. But both were slower than the financial grapevine. Somehow the news of the Treasury sale reached the Gold Room ahead of either telegram. Likely some speculators had spies in one of the telegraph offices in Washington; if they didn't actually read Boutwell's message, they could have inferred its gist from the mere arrival of a messenger from the Treasury. Whatever the mode of transmission, the word flashed to the Gold Room. A reporter covering the scene described the climax of the bull market, and the events that followed.

Amid all the noise and confusion the penetrating voices of the leading brokers of the clique are still heard advancing the price at each bid, and increasing the amount of their bids at each advance, until at last, with voice overtopping the bedlam below, the memorable bid burst forth, "160 for any part of five millions." . . . The noise was hushed. Terror became depicted on every countenance. Cool, sober men, looked at one another, and noted the ashy paleness that spread all over. Even those who had but little or no interest at stake were seized with the infection of fear and were conscious of a great evil approaching. And from the silence again came forth that shrieking bid, "160 for five millions," and no answer. "161 for five millions." "162 for five millions." Still no answer. "162 for any part of five millions." And a quiet voice said, "Sold one million at 162."

That quiet voice broke the fascination. The bid of 162 was not renewed. But 161 was again bid for a million, and the same quiet voice said, "Sold." And the bid of 161 was not renewed. But 160 was again bid for five millions. Then it dimly dawned upon the quicker witted that for some reason or other the game was up. As if by magnetic sympathy the same thought passed through the crowd at once. A dozen men leapt furiously at the bidder, and claimed to have sold the whole five millions. To their horror the bidder stood his ground and declared he would take all. But before the words had fairly passed his lips, before the terror at his action had had time to gain men's hearts, there was a rush amid the crowd. New men, wild with fresh excitement, crowded to the barriers. In an instant the rumor was abroad: the Treasury is selling. Quick as thought, men realized that it was not safe to sell to the clique brokers. Scarcely any one now wanted to buy. All who had bought were mad to sell at any price, but there were no buyers. In less time than it takes to write about it, the price fell from 162 to 135. The great gigantic bubble had burst, and half Wall Street was involved in ruin.

The ruined half now turned on those they perceived as the authors of their calamity: Fisk and Gould. The partners were forced to flee the financial district for their lives. An eyewitness contended that had the masterminds of the gold corner been caught by the victims of its collapse, "the chances were that the lamp-post near by would have very soon been decorated with a breathless body." Gould and Fisk made it to the Opera House, where they took refuge behind a cordon of bodyguards retained for just such emergencies.

What the partners said to each other, as they caught their breath in their marble sanctum, only they knew. "Nothing is lost save honor," Gould had pronounced at a critical moment of the Erie War; perhaps he encouraged Fisk similarly now. Or perhaps they were too busy fending off the maddened investors to pause for reflection. Fisk thought Gould looked terrible. "He has no courage at all," Fisk told an associate. "He has sunk right down. There is nothing left of him but a heap of clothes and a pair of eyes." At some later point, Fisk discovered that Gould had anticipated the break and been secretly selling, but for the time being, as the panic from the collapsed corner spread from the money market to the stock market and rippled into the broader economy, they continued their separate affairs. "It was each man drag out his own corpse," Fisk said.

5

The Transit of Jupiter

isk and Gould survived Black Friday, as that dire session became known, to fight another day. They surrounded themselves with lawyers to supplement the thugs at the Opera House; the law men threw up a cloud of litigation that kept the pair's creditors at a distance for months and in several cases years, until even the most indefatigable victims of the gold conspiracy finally settled. The two returned to railroading, working together until Fisk met a bloody end at the hands of a rival in love, who murdered him in 1872 on the staircase of the Grand Central Hotel on Broadway in Manhattan. Fisk went out in characteristic style; a hundred thousand people jammed the streets for his funeral parade, which featured an honor guard of New York's Ninth Militia Regiment and a brass band. Gould lived another two decades and became almost respectable as a railroad magnate and telegraph-company owner. But some people couldn't forgive him for his raid on gold, and when he died in 1892 he wasn't mourned. "There was no sorrow by his bier," the *New York World* reported. "There was decent respect—nothing more."

THE OTHER JAY—Jay Cooke—also survived the gold panic, but barely. The Civil War bond seller had distrusted the gold speculators since dark moments of the war, when the gold bulls had cheered the Union reverses that made the dollar dive. After the war Cooke encouraged the Treasury to retire the greenbacks and return the country to the gold standard; failing this, he said, the government should orchestrate gold sales so as "to keep things steady for the honest interests of the country." In 1869 Cooke and brother Henry were among those urging the Treasury to sell gold to counter the Gould-Fisk gold spike, in part from principle and in part because Cooke & Company had gone short in gold, believing the corner couldn't be sustained. Henry Cooke subsequently claimed it was *his* influence that caused Boutwell to sell the Treasury gold and break the corner. If true, this was a dubious accomplishment, for the Treasury-induced collapse of the gold price nearly swamped the Cookes along with everyone else. Another brother, Pitt Cooke, headed the bailing efforts. "I have been writing up our side of the Gold muddle," Pitt told Jay, "until I can demonstrate that black is white (in all cases except Jim Fisk and the devil)." Jay gave orders to batten down the hatches. "Get in every dollar you can, and loan only on what is instant cash."

The gold panic prompted Cooke to turn in another direction. The recent completion of the first transcontinental railroad—the Union Pacific–Central Pacific combination, from Omaha to

Sacramento—inspired emulators, and Cooke linked up with a group projecting a northern line, from Lake Superior to Puget Sound. Like the Union and Central Pacifics, Cooke's Northern Pacific would rely on land grants from the federal government; these would provide the collateral to support the $100 million in construction bonds Cooke proposed to sell. Cooke applied the same energy and imagination to the marketing of the railroad bonds he had employed on behalf of the Union. He touted the region through which the Northern Pacific would run as the finest real estate in America. Duluth, he said, would rival Chicago as the great city of the West. (This claim acquired a certain credibility when much of Chicago burned to the ground in 1871.) The Red River Valley of Dakota would grow the grain that would feed the world; the plains of Montana would supply the beef. The headwaters of the Yellowstone, with their geysers and hot springs, were a tourists' wonderland. The Cascade Mountains of Washington held timber that would build houses for a nation of a hundred million. The sheltered harbor of Puget Sound made San Francisco seem a roadstead. Cooke's promotions pumped bond sales; they also inspired snickers among those comparative few who had actually *been* to the region in question and who derisively dubbed it "Cooke's banana belt."

Unluckily for Cooke, the campaign for the Northern Pacific coincided with revelations of spectacular corruption in the building of the Union Pacific. Bondholders had been fleeced by an inside crew—calling itself Crédit Mobilier—that left the larger corporation holding the debt while the insiders skimmed the profits. The Crédit Mobilier scandal, combined with further shenanigans on the Erie Railroad, spoiled the market for railroad bonds, and Cooke found himself suddenly illiquid. "Owing to unexpected demands on us, our firm has been obliged to suspend payment," he posted on the door at 114 South Third Street on September 18, 1873.

"A thunderclap in a clear sky," the *Philadelphia Press* described the announcement. Not since the closing of Nicholas Biddle's bank three decades earlier had the financial community experienced such a blow. "If I had been struck on the head with a hammer, I could not have been more stunned," one old-timer explained. "I rubbed my eyes to see if I was quite awake. . . . It seemed as though the ground had passed from under foot and the stars had gone from the sky." Cooke & Company's failure touched off a mad run on banks in Philadelphia, New York, and Boston; the weaker fell at once, the stronger somewhat later. The Panic of 1873 proved the worst since before the Civil War—the worst, by some measures, since the 1837 panic that followed the Jackson-Biddle Bank War. Thousands of financial institutions and other companies closed, leaving their employees bereft, their depositors and investors empty-handed, and the country wondering where all this money trouble would end.

JOHN PIERPONT MORGAN was a rarity among the money men of the nineteenth century: a person born to the business. His father, Junius Morgan, inherited a fortune from *his* father and used the capital to build a Boston brokerage of commodities and merchandise traded across the Atlantic. The business introduced Junius to Lombard Street, the world of London bankers, from whom he imbibed a philosophy articulated by Walter Bagehot, the founding editor of the *Economist* magazine. "The banker's calling is hereditary," Bagehot asserted, on the basis of his study of the Baring and Rothschild dynasties. "The credit of the bank descends from father to son; this inherited wealth brings inherited refinement." Junius bred Pierpont, as the son was called, to the money trade. The boy attended Boston's premier schools; after Junius relocated his offices to England, he sent Pierpont to Switzerland and then Germany to absorb the best education Europe had to offer. At the University of Göttingen the boy impressed his mathematics instructors with a flair for numbers. One of his professors urged him to stay on and join the mathematics faculty; Pierpont replied he would put his reckoning skills to work in the family calling.

He arrived on Wall Street during the panic season of 1857, which shook out much dead wood and left openings for newcomers. Morgan apprenticed with the firm that served as American agent for his father's company, and soon acted as though he owned the place. His audacity alarmed his employers, who declined to make him partner and thereby prompted him to go into competition with them. J. P. Morgan & Company opened in 1861 and instantly profited from the soaring demand for commodities during the Civil War. The return Morgan was required to file under the new tax law showed an income for 1864 of $50,000.

Morgan steered clear of the gold boom and bust of 1869, preferring to invest in railroads. These nearly proved his undoing during the Cooke panic of 1873. But Morgan wasn't quite as exposed as Cooke and many others, and when all the financial debris stopped falling, Morgan's house still stood, conspicuous among the rubble.

The 1873 panic suggested certain lessons, of which the most obvious was the need to reorganize the railroad industry. Morgan wasn't alone in thinking the industry overbuilt, that there were too many railroads chasing too little freight and too few passengers. But he was unusual, and eventually unique, in his ability to act on this insight. As part of his price for underwriting railroad issues, he insisted on seats for himself or his partners on the boards of directors of the issuing lines. The perspective these perches afforded him provided additional insight into the operation of the industry; before long he was the country's leading expert on railroads.

To rationalize the industry—to reduce the competition— became a Morgan mission. A brutal struggle had developed between the Pennsylvania Railroad and the New York Central. The Central invaded the Penn's territory by starting a line from Philadelphia to Pittsburgh; the Penn struck back by blasting a route that challenged the Central's dominance from New York to Buffalo. Morgan had a special stake in this fight, as the detonations by the Penn disrupted the peace of his Hudson River estate and the immigrant construction crews frightened his children. Morgan determined to end the Penn-Central war. He summoned the leaders of the Penn, Frank Thompson and George Roberts, to join him and fellow Central director Chauncey Depew aboard his yacht, the *Corsair*. The steamer and its passengers departed

Jersey City at ten o'clock the morning of the meeting and headed north. Thompson soon agreed with Morgan that a ceasefire made sense. The Penn would leave New York to the Central, and the Central would cede Pennsylvania to the Penn. Roberts, however, was more reluctant, and Depew—one of the great talkers of the era—worked him over all afternoon. The boat ascended nearly to West Point, then doubled back beyond its slip to Sandy Hook. Depew kept talking, and the cruise showed no sign of ending. Finally, worn down by Depew and perhaps fearing that Morgan would never put him ashore, Roberts relented. "I will agree to your plan and do my part," he said.

The "Corsair Compact" confirmed Morgan's mastery of railroading. The industry's leading association looked to him whenever competition became oppressive, and he responded by hosting summit meetings of the railroad presidents at his home in Manhattan's Murray Hill neighborhood. Financial reporters would trail the executives to Morgan's door; some peered into the windows with opera glasses while others dressed as deliverymen and rang the bell. The markets hung on the outcome of these sessions. Inside Morgan made plain why he had brought the railroaders there. "The purpose of this meeting is to cause the members of this association to no longer take the law into their own hands when they suspect they have been wronged," he announced at one such affair. "This is not elsewhere customary in civilized communities, and no good reason exists why such a practice should continue among railroads." Morgan persuaded the presidents that future financing for their roads required self-denial on their parts. Price competition must cease, and construction of new roads must be rational. Some of the railroaders occasionally balked, but most went along. "RAILROAD KINGS FORM A GIGANTIC TRUST," a typical next-day headline declared.

MORGAN'S RAILROAD WORK solved some of that industry's problems, but it left untouched larger issues of American finance. The price level declined relentlessly during the 1880s and early 1890s, partly on account of productivity improvements in industry and agriculture, and partly as a result of a shrinking money supply. In 1879, after great debate in Congress, the Treasury had resumed specie payments, redeeming greenbacks for gold, which became America's de facto standard. The dearer money warmed the hearts of creditors but left debtors shivering as their debts increased in real terms. America's gold standard—which was also the international standard—meanwhile rendered the American economy more vulnerable to the vagaries of foreign finance, and when speculative bubbles burst overseas, the instability spread to America.

A series of such foreign burstings in the early 1890s produced the Panic of 1893 in America. Twenty years of industrialization since the last panic meant millions more Americans now worked for wages; initial layoffs in manufacturing induced a widening downdraft as the unemployed defaulted on rents and stopped purchasing consumer goods. Within months the country experienced its first full-blown industrial depression.

Americans had never suffered so. "Men died like flies under the strain," Henry Adams recalled of New England. "Boston grew suddenly old, haggard, and thin." A railroad strike at Pullman, Illinois, called to protest wage cuts, spread until it paralyzed traffic in dozens of states. A disgruntled army of the unemployed, led by an Ohio Theosophist named Jacob Coxey, whose inflationist monetary theories inspired him to christen his son Legal Tender, marched on Washington demanding relief. "Never before has there been such a sudden and shaking cessation of industrial activity," the *Commercial and Financial Chronicle* reported. "Mills, factories, furnaces, mines nearly everywhere shut down in large numbers. . . . Hundreds of thousands of men thrown out of employment." Sober observers of American society feared general unrest, perhaps civil war. "In no civilized country in this century, not actually in the throes of war or open insurrection, has society been so disorganized as it was in the United States during the first half of 1894," an editor declared a short while later. "Never was human life held so cheap. Never did the constituted authorities appear so incompetent to enforce respect for law."

THE TURMOIL PRODUCED numerous schemes and projects for mitigating the distress. Many of these focused on the money question, which seemed to lie at the heart of the problem, even if the various schemers and projectors couldn't agree on its angle of repose. None of the public commentators produced a greater effect than a remarkable young man who conducted a "school of finance" in Chicago, at the Art Institute there. "Coin" used but the single name, and no one knew anything about his background or even his age, although he appeared quite young. He entered public view on May 7, 1894, when he opened his school and essayed "to instruct the youths of the nation with a view to their having a clear understanding of what has been considered an abstruse subject; to lead them out of the labyrinth of falsehoods, heresies and isms that distract the country." After greeting the class and specifying the ground rules—all questions answered, nothing accepted on faith—Coin cut straight to the point. "My object will be to teach you the A, B, C of the questions about money that are now a matter of every-day conversation."

Coin commenced the lecture proper. "In money there must be a unit," he explained. In arithmetic the unit was the number 1, which he wrote on the blackboard with a confident stroke. The monetary unit was the dollar, fixed by Congress in 1792 as containing 371¼ grains of fine silver. Gold was also denominated as money, Coin said, "but its value was counted from these silver units or dollars." The ratio of silver to gold was originally 15 to 1, later 16 to 1. For eighty years the United States maintained this bimetallic standard, with Americans free to choose between the two metals. Ordinary people preferred silver, Coin said, because it was the most reliable. "It was scattered among all the people. Men having a design to injure business by making money scarce could not so easily get hold of all the silver and hide it away, as they could gold. . . . Gold was considered the money of the rich. It was owned principally by that class of people, and the poor people seldom handled it." Silver was the more democratic. "It was so much handled by the people and preferred by them, that it was called the people's money."

There matters rested until 1873, when Congress passed an

act revising the country's coinage laws. This act made gold the unit of value and discontinued the minting of silver dollars. The deed was done stealthily, Coin said, and he quoted a senator who compared its passage to the "silent tread of a cat." Yet the consequence could scarcely be overstated. "An army of a half million men invading our shores, the warships of the world bombarding our coasts, could not have made us surrender the money of the people and substitute in its place the money of the rich. . . . The pen was mightier than the sword."

To explicate the evil impact of the 1873 law, Coin reviewed the basic relationship between money and the items for which it was traded. "The value of the property of the world, as expressed in money, depends on what money is made of, and how much money there is. . . . If the quantity of money is large, the total value of the property of the world will be correspondingly large as expressed in dollars or money units. If the quantity of money is small, the total value of the property of the world will be correspondingly reduced." By demonetizing silver in 1873, Congress had effectively reduced the supply of money, which now depended on the amount of gold in the country. Coin summoned two assistants to demonstrate a striking point. The young men measured off on the stage a square twenty-two feet on each side. They then raised a stick twenty-two feet long into a vertical position. Coin requested the audience to imagine a cube of the measured dimensions. *That space will hold all the gold in the world obtainable for use as money!*" he said.

The audience gasped in disbelief. Coin let the lesson sink in, then pushed on. "It is in this quantity of gold that it is proposed to measure the value of all the other property in the world," he said. "Its significance is written in our present low prices and depression in business."

The advocates of gold as the sole basis for American money knew what they were doing, Coin asserted. Typically creditors, they magnified the value of their credits by constraining the money supply within that twenty-two-foot cube. Debtors and other ordinary people paid the price in their falling standard of living—which would continue to fall if the money men had their way. The republic itself was in peril. Coin pointed to the imagined cube of gold.

One pinch from that block of gold the size of a gold dollar— one twentieth of an ounce—will be so valuable that it will not only buy two bushels of wheat, as it does now, but it will then buy four bushels of wheat. One half that quantity will buy ten hours' labor from a strong-armed mechanic. So much as you could put in the palm of your hand will then buy a man's soul— a statesman's honor. It is breaking down the fabric of our institutions, driving hope from the heart and happiness from the minds of our people. Who can estimate the damage to the commerce and business of the world? Who can estimate the suffering that humanity has and must yet experience? In what language can we characterize the men behind the scenes who knowingly are directing the world to the gold standard?

Coin returned to the event—the revision of the coinage law— that had set the dire train in motion. "It is commonly known as the *crime of 1873*," he said. "A crime because it has confiscated millions of dollars worth of property. A crime because it has made thousands of paupers. A crime because it has made tens of thousands tramps. A crime because it has made thousands of suicides. . . . A crime because it has brought this once great republic to the verge of ruin, where it is now in danger of tottering to its fall." The victims of the crime were peculiarly the men and women of the West, where debtors were many and creditors few. Coin showed a drawing of a giant sponge hovering over the Appalachians. The sponge sopped up the resources of the farmers of the West and squeezed them out upon the bankers of the East. This damaged the debtors individually but also their communities. "When your neighbor has sent all of his money off, he has none left to spend with you."

There was an international angle to the thievery, as well. The Bank of England had been pressing gold upon the world for decades. America's money men were simply doing England's bidding. Some professed impotence, declaring the forces of world finance to be beyond American control. Coin thought these faint-hearts had things just backward. "If it is claimed we must adopt for our money the metal England selects, and can have no independent choice in the matter, let us make the test and find out if it is true. It is not American to give up without trying. If it is true, let us attach England to the United States and blot her name out from among the nations of the earth." At this the audience applauded loudly. Coin continued, "A war with England would be the most popular ever waged on the face of the earth." More applause. "If it is true that she can dictate the money of the

world and thereby create world-wide misery, it would be the most
just war ever waged by man." Cheers and shouts.

But it needn't come to that, Coin assured his listeners.
Americans could reclaim their own destiny by remonetizing silver and restoring the balance to American money.

> Give the people back their favored primary money! Give us
> two arms with which to transact business! Silver the right arm,
> and gold the left arm! Silver the money of the people, and gold
> the money of the rich. Stop this legalized robbery that is trans-
> ferring the property of the debtors to the possession of the
> creditors!
>
> Citizens! The integrity of the government has been vio-
> lated. A financial trust has control of your money, and with it
> is robbing you of your property. Vampires feed upon your com-
> mercial blood. . . . Oppression now seeks to enslave this fair
> land. Its name is greed. . . . This is a struggle for humanity—
> for our homes and firesides, for the purity and integrity of our
> government.

With every sentence, the audience cheered, more enthusiastically each time. Coin kept them just shy of bedlam as he told a
story of Benjamin Franklin after the Revolutionary War, dining
with diplomats from England and France. The English diplomat
proposed a toast to England, which he likened to the sun as giving light to the world. The French diplomat toasted France as the
moon that controlled the motion of the tides. Franklin toasted
the United States: "the Joshua that commanded the sun and

moon to stand still—and they *stood still*." Coin declared that this must be the attitude of Americans on the contemporary money question. "If we had an administration and Congress now that would say to England, 'Stand still,' one loud shout would be heard in this country from sea to sea and Lakes to Gulf, proclaiming the second independence of the United States."

Coin's listeners could contain themselves no longer. They roared their assent and crowded the stage, each striving to shake his hand and slap his back. Chicago had never witnessed such a bravura performance, and few of those present expected to witness its like again.

AN ENCORE WAS especially improbable given that the original performance never actually occurred. Coin was the invention of William Harvey, a Virginian too young to have fought in the Civil War but old enough to remember the way it had split the western part of the Old Dominion—Harvey's part—from the tidewater east. Harvey bounced around the Ohio Valley before migrating west to the silver district of Colorado, where he managed a mine for three years, until the falling price of silver—in part the result of demonetization in 1873—forced him to seek other work. He hawked patent medicine and promoted a tourist stop in Pueblo that featured the gems and precious metals of the Rockies; after hearing that Chicago was to host a world's fair in 1893 he headed there. He arrived in time for the Panic of 1893—another consequence, he judged, of the decision to drop silver—and, lacking better prospects amid the depression that followed, he decided to take the case for silver to the people.

The literature on the money question in the 1890s included treatises as abstruse as financial tracts had ever been, but also oversimplifications, partisan polemics, and conspiracy theories. Harvey's genius was to join the arcane to the simplistic and the bombastic. His "Coin" was very young, to show that the money question wasn't really complicated once one got past the interested arguments of the bankers and the gold bugs. Harvey illustrated the printed version of Coin's lectures—the only version that existed—with cartoons that amplified the pro-silver arguments of the text. John Sherman, an author of the 1873 coinage law, was shown wielding a pen that decapitated the maiden Silver. A one-legged man represented the American economy after the cutoff of silver. An enormous cow grazed on western corn while eastern bankers milked it and hauled the pails to England. The tentacles of an octopus named "Rothschild" spanned the earth and drew the wealth of every region into its capacious maw. Skeletons behind the bars of a crypt labeled "Gold Standard" had obviously ignored the warning above the door: "All ye who enter here, leave hope behind."

Harvey, when pressed, never pretended Coin actually existed. But many of the million who bought his small book—*Coin's Financial School*—apparently believed Coin was real. The gold advocates felt obliged to rebut the imaginary wunderkind. *Coin's Financial Fool, The Mistakes of Coin, Coin at School in Finance, The Closing Days of Coin's Financial School, Cash vs. Coin,* and numerous other titles pointed out that apathy rather than conspiracy explained the terms of the Coinage Act of 1873 (silver producers, able to get more for their metal on the open market, had simply stopped delivering silver to the mint), that global overproduction of wheat and other commodities had as much to do with falling prices as the demonetization of silver (American farmers now competed with farmers in Argentina, Russia, and other countries), that a decision by the United States to remonetize silver would almost certainly fall flat if other countries didn't follow suit (money flowed across oceans even faster than wheat did), that the free coinage of silver at the 16-to-1 ratio of silver to gold favored by the Coinites would be hair-raisingly inflationary (the market ratio was about 32 to 1), that much of the heft behind the silver movement came from well-heeled silver-mine owners (rather than from the "people").

Harvey answered his critics in subsequent editions of *Coin's Financial School*. He might have saved his ink. For all the trappings of monetary theory in which he couched his message, Harvey's appeal was chiefly to the heart. Gold and silver were simply the latest proxies in the historic contest between capitalism and democracy, between wealth and commonwealth. Harvey understood this, as he revealed in closing his account of the Coin lectures. "In the struggle of might against right," he wrote, "the former has generally triumphed. Will it win in the United States?"

SEVERAL MONTHS AFTER Coin purportedly lectured in Chicago, J. P. Morgan genuinely boarded his private rail car for a trip to Washington. Since the 1893 panic, the Treasury's gold supply had been dwindling. Conventional wisdom considered

$100 million the minimum the government needed to ensure liq-
uidity in the face of demands by foreigners and others who
insisted on redeeming Treasury notes for the yellow metal that
backed them. This number was financially arbitrary but psycho-
logically significant: if investors believed a dip below $100 mil-
lion was cause for alarm, the belief alone could make it so.

The investors grew nervous as 1894 ended with the federal
coffers holding barely more than the magic $100 million. A New
Year's rally brought a slight respite, but then a post-holiday fit of
pessimism sent the reserve plunging, to $68 million on January
24, 1895. Dollar-holders hastened, then sprinted headlong, to
the Treasury to redeem their notes, and the reserve dove further,
to $45 million on January 31 and less than $10 million on
February 2. The United States, by all evidence, would be forced
off the gold standard within days, perhaps hours.

President Grover Cleveland didn't know what to do. "I have
been dreadfully forlorn these many months, and sorely per-
plexed and tried," he wrote a friend. Cleveland was a gold man,
unlike an increasing number of his fellow Democrats. He
believed a return to silver would ruin the country, making it a
laughingstock among the trading states of the world. But he
realized he might have no alternative to silver if the government
ran out of gold.

Cleveland detected a single means of escape, though it made
him sweat merely to think of it. J. P. Morgan could rescue the
government, if anyone could. But Cleveland didn't like Morgan,
and he liked the implications of a deal with Morgan even less.
Morgan stood for everything Democrats (and their Jeffersonian

Republican ancestors) had abhorred since the days of Hamilton
and Biddle: big money, big business, and the excessive influence
they wielded over the lives of ordinary people. "Jupiter" Morgan,
as he was commonly called, might save the Treasury, but the
price could be democracy's soul.

While Cleveland sweated, Morgan made himself available.
He hitched his rail car to a southbound train and rode to
Washington. He was met at Union Station by Daniel Lamont,
Cleveland's secretary of war and closest friend in the capital.
Morgan expected to receive an invitation to the White House; he
was surprised to hear Lamont say Cleveland would *not* see him.
Any communications would have to take place indirectly.

Morgan found this unacceptable and said so. "I have come
down to Washington to see the President," he told Lamont. "And
I am going to stay here until I see him." He hailed a carriage and
proceeded to the home of a longtime friend. He received callers
till midnight, and then played solitaire before retiring.

He was eating breakfast the next morning when word arrived
that Cleveland had changed his mind. He would see Morgan
after all. Morgan cut across Lafayette Square to the executive
mansion, where he was ushered directly to the president's office.
Cleveland joined him shortly. They spoke of the financial crisis
but in language, on Cleveland's part, that suggested to Morgan
that the president didn't understand just how dire the situation
had become. Morgan stated the matter as starkly as he could. He
had learned that a single investor held a draft for $10 million
against the Treasury's gold reserve, which currently hovered
around $9 million. "If that $10 million draft is presented, you

can't meet it," Morgan told Cleveland. "It will be all over before three o'clock."

Cleveland now understood. "What suggestion have you to make, Mr. Morgan?" he replied.

Morgan explained that a public bond offering, toward which some in the Treasury were leaning, would fail, as it would take too long. Something swifter was necessary. Morgan recommended a private sale, to a syndicate headed by himself, which would pay for the bonds in gold coin. Cleveland questioned his own authority for ordering such a sale. Morgan replied that a Civil War statute—number "four thousand and something"— had authorized President Lincoln to make emergency bond sales; if the statute was still in force, it ought to suffice. The president turned to Richard Olney, his attorney general, and inquired whether this was so. Olney said he'd have to look it up. He left the room, and returned moments later with a volume of the Revised Statutes. He handed it to the Treasury secretary, John Carlisle, who read aloud, "The Secretary of the Treasury may purchase coin with any of the bonds or notes of the United States . . . upon such terms as he may deem most advantageous to the public interest." Carlisle looked at Cleveland. "Mr. President," he said, "that seems to fit the situation exactly."

Morgan suggested an issue of $100 million, which would signal the government's seriousness by putting the reserve back above the safety mark. Cleveland balked. Sixty million would have to do, he said. He then pressed Morgan for assurance that the bond sale would accomplish what it was supposed to. "Mr. Morgan, what guarantee have we that if we adopt this plan, gold

will not continue to be shipped abroad, and while we are getting
it in, it will go out, and we will not reach our goal? Will you guarantee that this will not happen?"

Cleveland was asking a lot—in essence, that Morgan stand
against the world to defend the credit of the United States.
Morgan didn't flinch. "Yes, sir," he said. "I will guarantee it during
the life of the syndicate, and that means until the contract has
been concluded and the goal has been reached."

It was a breathtaking promise, one only Morgan among
American financiers could give with a straight face. But
Cleveland took him at his word, and the deal was struck. As the
group rose to go to lunch, one of Morgan's associates pointed to
some brownish dust on the carpet about his feet. All required a
moment to realize that the dust was the tobacco of an unlit cigar
Morgan had silently ground to powder during the discussion.

THE MORGAN DEAL rescued the Treasury but won neither
Cleveland nor Morgan any friends. Populist-minded Democrats
screamed that the president had sold out democracy to the capitalists; Congress summoned Morgan to testify before a committee investigating the inside deal. The interrogators demanded to
know what profit Morgan and his syndicate made from the government's distress.

"That I decline to answer," Morgan said. "I am perfectly ready
to state to the committee every detail of the negotiation up to the
time that the bonds became my property and were paid for. What
I did with my own property subsequent to that purchase I

decline to state." And he continued to decline, despite repeated efforts to squeeze the information out of him.

Cleveland's complicity with Morgan, and Morgan's disdain for democratic oversight of private finance, made it nearly inevitable that the Democratic nomination for president in 1896 would go to the most radically anti-capitalist of the credible contenders. William Jennings Bryan sealed his convention victory with a stirring speech that outdid anything on the money question since the demagogic days of Thomas Hart Benton. Bryan had represented Nebraska in Congress before the depression-year elections of 1894 swept scores of the majority Democratic incumbents away ("Their dead will be buried in trenches and marked 'Unknown,'" Republican Thomas Reed chortled). Bryan traveled the country the next two years, shaking hands, stumping for candidates, and spreading the gospel of silver. As the Democrats gathered in Chicago in July 1896 to nominate a successor to Cleveland, Bryan prepared to challenge the still regnant gold Democrats associated with the administration, who hoped to engineer the nomination of a sound-money man like the president.

The uprising began at once. "The silver men are running this affair," Ben Tillman of South Carolina shouted, in words that were more assertive than descriptive at the time he spoke. "And they propose to do it in their own fashion. If the gold men don't like it, let them bolt. I hope they will." The intensity of emotion among the radical silverites shocked the gold conservatives. "For the first time, I can understand the scenes of the French revolution," one said. Another mused ominously, "Perhaps somewhere in this country there lurks a Robespierre, a Danton, a Marat?" A mournful member of the old guard was asked why he didn't smile and look pleasant for the photographers. "I never smile and look pleasant at a funeral," he answered.

A brawl erupted over the platform, with the radicals gaining an edge. "We of the South have burned our bridges behind us so far as the Eastern Democrats are concerned," Tillman of South Carolina declared. "We denounce the administration of President Cleveland as undemocratic and tyrannical." The platform committee called for new monetary policies to restore democracy and defeat tyranny. "We are unalterably opposed to monometallism, which has locked fast the prosperity of an industrial people in the paralysis of hard times," the draft platform proclaimed. "We demand the free and unlimited coinage of both silver and gold at the present legal ratio of 16 to 1."

The inclusion of this plank touched off a debate in the convention as a whole, which climaxed when Nebraska's Bryan took the stage. The silverites yelled and stamped approval at his mere appearance. He calmed them by starting quietly. He was young and untested, he granted. Others in the party knew more about certain policies. Yet he offered his honest convictions, which ought to count for something. "The humblest citizen in all the land, when clad in the armor of a righteous cause, is stronger than all the hosts of error. I come to speak to you in defense of a cause as holy as the cause of liberty—the cause of humanity."

The audience absorbed the rhythms of Bryan's voice. "At the close of a sentence, it would rise and shout, and when I began upon another sentence, the room was as still as a church," Bryan recalled later. "I thought of a choir, as I noted how instantaneously and in unison they responded to each point made."

After a bit more preface, Bryan ripped into the gold men for slandering the cause of silver. The capitalists claimed that the silverites were disturbing the business interests of the country.

> We reply that *you* have disturbed *our* business interests by your course. We say to you that *you* have made the definition of a business man too limited in its application. The man who is employed for wages is as much a business man as his employer; the attorney in a country town is as much a business man as the corporation counsel in a great metropolis; the merchant at the crossroads store is as much a business man as the merchant of New York; the farmer who goes forth in the morning and toils all day, who begins in the spring and toils all summer, and who by the application of brain and muscle to the natural resources of the country creates wealth, is as much a business man as the man who goes upon the board of trade and bets upon the price of grain. . . . We come to speak of this broader class of business men.

Bryan claimed the patron saints of the Democratic party for his cause. Jefferson had opposed Hamilton on the money question. "I stand with Jefferson," Bryan said. Jackson had fought Biddle over the Bank of the United States. "He destroyed the bank conspiracy and saved America." The gold men today were as wrong as the big capitalists had always been. "There are two ideas of government. There are those who believe that if you will only legislate to make the well-to-do prosperous, their prosperity will leak through on those below. The democratic idea, however, has been that if you legislate to make the masses prosperous, their prosperity will find its way up through every class which rests upon them."

The advocates of silver were charged with radicalism, with assaulting the temple of respectability. Bryan denied the charge, saying the silver men were the true conservatives. "We are fighting in defense of our homes, our families, our posterity." And fight they would, for they had no choice. "We have petitioned, and our petitions have been scorned. We have entreated, and our entreaties have been disregarded. We have begged, and they have mocked when our calamity came. We beg no more. We entreat no more. We petition no more. *We defy them!*"

The crowd thundered its approval. Even some of the gold delegates, caught in the riptide of Bryan's rhetoric, began cheering the speaker. Many delegates, thinking the speech was over, started to storm the stage, to carry Bryan bodily off.

Bryan basked in the tumult, then stilled it. He wasn't done. The gold standard yet stood. "You come and tell us that the great cities are in favor of the gold standard. We reply that the great cities rest upon our broad and fertile prairies. Burn down your cities and leave our farms, and your cities will spring up again as if by magic. But destroy our farms and the grass will grow in the streets of every city in the country." The money men said America couldn't change the currency alone, that any alteration in money required the cooperation of England and the other trading countries. Bryan refused to bow to Britain. "It is the issue of 1776 over again. Our ancestors, when but three millions in num-

H. W. Brands

ber, had the courage to declare their political independence. . . .
Shall we, their descendants, when we have grown to seventy millions, declare that we are less independent than our forefathers?"

The lines had been drawn. The battle was joined. The money
men took one side, the people the other.

> If they dare to come out in the open field and defend the gold
> standard as a good thing, we will fight them to the uttermost.
> Having behind us the producing masses of this nation and the
> world, supported by the commercial interests, the laboring
> interests, and the toilers everywhere, we will answer their
> demand for a gold standard by saying to them: You shall not
> press down upon the brow of labor this crown of thorns! You
> shall not crucify mankind upon a cross of gold!

WITH THIS SPEECH Bryan won the nomination and framed the
election. Not since 1832, when Jackson vetoed Biddle, had
the money question so dominated a presidential campaign. The
Populist party, which had raised the silver issue in the first place,
seconded Bryan's nomination, despite the fears of many Populists
that doing so would deprive the party of its raison d'être. Gold
Democrats groused, with many hoping for Bryan's defeat. The
smaller group of silver Republicans, most with ties to silver mines
or the states where they were located, sat on their hands while
Republican boss Mark Hanna directed the campaign of William
McKinley, the Ohio governor with a solid record of being friendly
to business and twenty-four karat on the money question.

Bryan's battle was uphill the whole way. Though opinions differed on the causes of the continuing depression, none could deny its effects, and voters trooped to the polls with a mind to punish the party that held the White House. Bryan preached silver, but McKinley—or rather his proxies, as he stayed home in Canton, Ohio—promised prosperity. Bryan's appeal to agrarian values galvanized the West and South but left the industrializing Northeast and Midwest indifferent. Some manufacturers allegedly told employees not to bother reporting to work in the event of a Bryan victory. That it didn't come even close to that reflected how much the country had changed since Jackson's day. Old Hickory could count on farmers and their friends for a winning majority; Bryan could not. He carried the farm districts by a large margin but lost the Northeast and Ohio Valley and, with them, the election. "God's in his heaven; all's right with the world," Hanna wired McKinley.

THE REPUBLICAN VICTORY—a gold Congress rode to Washington on McKinley's coattails—settled the money question for the moment. But what scuttled silver forever were subsequent developments beyond the reach of politics. New discoveries of gold in South Africa and the Yukon and new techniques for stripping gold from ore dramatically expanded the world gold supply, accomplishing some of the inflationary objectives of the silverites without resort to their favorite metal. The return of prosperity under McKinley—which had more to do with the business cycle than with the composition of money—

further eroded demand for drastic remedies. The Gold Standard Act of 1900, followed by McKinley's reelection the same year, ratified the monetary policy he espoused.

The country entered the new century with cause for capitalist celebration. J. P. Morgan did his part by underwriting the establishment of the mammoth United States Steel Corporation. Capitalized in 1901 at $1.4 billion, the steel trust summarized the power of Morgan and the money he controlled. A few months later he godfathered a railroad trust, the Northern Securities Company, which married Jay Cooke's old Northern Pacific to the newer Great Northern line of James J. Hill. Nothing, it seemed, was beyond the reach of the greatest money man in American history.

But then things began to go wrong. McKinley was assassinated in Buffalo, leaving the White House to Theodore Roosevelt, whose devotion to capitalism was considerably less certain than McKinley's. Mark Hanna had feared such a development and for this reason had resisted Roosevelt's addition to the ticket in 1900. "Don't any of you realize," Hanna bellowed, "that there's only one life between that madman and the presidency?" Hanna and other skeptics weren't mollified when Roosevelt promised, shortly after taking office, to carry out the policies of his predecessor. Carry them out the way trash men carry out the garbage, the distrusters said.

They seemed to be right when Roosevelt took the utterly un-McKinleyan step of attacking Morgan's Northern Securities. In 1902 the Justice Department, at Roosevelt's direction, initiated antitrust proceedings against the railroad combine. Morgan was outraged. Since his rescue of the Treasury in 1895, he had come to consider himself indispensable to the republic, a fourth branch of government. He didn't expect the other branches to agree with him on all things, but he certainly expected to be consulted. Roosevelt sprang his attack by stealth; Morgan could have told him the stock market would react by swooning, which it did.

As he had with Cleveland, Morgan traveled to Washington and insisted on seeing the president. Roosevelt invited him in at once. Morgan came straight to the point. "If we have done something wrong," he said, "send your man to my man, and they can fix it up."

"That can't be done," Roosevelt replied. Philander Knox, Roosevelt's attorney general and the lead prosecutor in the Northern Securities case, explained, "We don't want to fix it up. We want to stop it."

Morgan eyed the president suspiciously. "Are you going to attack my other interests? The steel trust and the others?"

"Certainly not," Roosevelt responded, "unless we find that in any case they have done something that we regard as wrong."

Morgan returned to New York and the prosecution proceeded, culminating in the breakup of Northern Securities. But Roosevelt stuck to his word. He didn't go after the steel trust, and he didn't try to bring Morgan down. He was content to assert a principle: that though money might govern the marketplace, the people ruled the public square. Roosevelt wasn't a foe of capitalism per se—though he regularly railed at the "criminal rich"— but he was an ardent defender of democracy.

Yet even Roosevelt was finally compelled to admit that the country couldn't do without the money men. Roosevelt's epiphany occurred in 1907, when another financial panic set in. The trouble started overseas, as it had the last time Morgan was called to the rescue. Gold production, after rising sharply in the late 1890s, failed to keep pace with world industrial output, and by the middle of the next decade several countries were feeling the pinch. An expensive war between Russia and Japan, followed by the 1906 earthquake and fire in San Francisco, added to the competition for capital and drove interest rates to record highs. London lenders got nearly seven percent from their most credit-worthy customers at the beginning of 1907. The foreign demand for capital drained gold from the United States, pushing several American banks and trust companies to the brink of insolvency. A failed attempt by speculators to corner the copper market reproduced some of the gyrations of Jay Gould's Black Friday and drove several bankers over the edge.

The signal collapse—the equivalent of Jay Cooke's closing in 1873—came on October 22 when the Knickerbocker Trust Company of New York couldn't meet its calls. Partly for the trivial reason of its distinctive name, the Knickerbocker was one of the best-known firms on Wall Street; its closing produced a panic that threatened to outdo the one of 1873.

This time, though, a steady and powerful hand provided a stabilizing force. That evening Morgan convened the leading bankers of New York at the Hotel Manhattan. George Cortelyou, Roosevelt's Treasury secretary, hurried up from Washington to join them. Morgan sufficiently impressed Cortelyou with the gravity of the situation that the secretary agreed on the spot to deliver $6 million to a syndicate Morgan was just then putting together. There would be more where this came from, should more be necessary. "The Secretary of the Treasury . . . will not hesitate to deal promptly and adequately with any situation that may arise," the administration announced.

Morgan had caught cold some days earlier, and the late meeting and general stress left him too tired to play his bedtime solitaire. The city awoke the next morning expecting the great money man to dispense credit and reassurance. But the Morgan mansion showed no sign of life as the hour of bank openings approached. Herbert Satterlee, a business intimate (and Morgan's son-in-law), voiced the alarm many others felt: "If he could not be aroused, the consequences were too serious to contemplate." Satterlee checked on Morgan, and discovered to his relief that it was merely the cold, worsened overnight, that had kept him abed.

Morgan drove to his office, where beleaguered bank presidents were already lined up. One by one he heard them out, reckoning their strengths and weaknesses. He changed venue in the afternoon, to the Morgan Library, where the audiences continued. He fell asleep during one session, and snored for half an hour. No one had the nerve to wake him. Morgan generally shunned publicity and kept his business as far from public view as possible, but now he let himself be seen with his fellow bankers. His aura alone lifted spirits. "There goes the Old Man!" cabbies called hopefully as he passed. Police stopped traffic to let him through.

His calm demeanor stabilized the situation, but only briefly. Fear spread from the money market to the stock market, where prices plunged in heavy trading. At one-thirty on October 24 the president of the New York Stock Exchange, R. H. Thomas, bolted into Morgan's office and declared that the exchange would have to close.

"What?" Morgan demanded.

"We will have to close the Stock Exchange," Thomas repeated.

Morgan's brow furrowed. "What time do you usually close it?" he said, as if he didn't know.

"Three o'clock."

"It must not close one minute before that hour today!" Morgan commanded.

Thomas said he had no choice. Money had vanished, leaving nothing to support prices. In their free-fall they were taking

J. P. Morgan didn't like candid photos, and the more candid the less he liked them.

down one brokerage after another. Morgan answered that he would find the money to keep the exchange open. He summoned the bank presidents back to his office, lectured them sternly, and within minutes pulled $27 million from their pockets. The news of this relief fund was telephoned to the stock exchange, where the brokers nearly rioted in gratitude, clamoring to get their hands on the money. The exchange stayed open.

As Morgan left the meeting, reporters crowded about. Did he have a message for the people of New York and America? Morgan answered distinctly: "If people will keep their money in the banks, everything will be all right."

But people *weren't* keeping their money in the banks, scores of which faced collapse. To alleviate the pressure, Morgan gathered the bankers again and got them to accept scrip—in essence IOUs—in their reciprocal transactions in order that the strong banks support the weak ones. The only authority Morgan had for this action was his financial prestige and his reputation for never forgetting who helped in time of trouble and who shirked.

A unexpected wrinkle in the crisis emerged when the city government of New York couldn't sell bonds it needed to cover operating expenses. Morgan assumed responsibility for the sale but in return demanded oversight of city spending. City officials acquiesced, albeit nervously.

Morgan plugged the final hole in the dike in a meeting in the Morgan Library. The presidents of New York's principal trust companies couldn't come to terms on a fund to support their struggling brethren. Morgan insisted they keep trying, and to encourage persistence he locked all the doors, preventing escape. As the cigar smoke thickened and the claustrophobia mounted, an agreement eventually hove into sight. A last hold-out, Edward King of the Union Trust, hesitated as he approached the document delineating the pact. Morgan gruffly guided him home. "Here's the place, King," he said, pointing to the line that awaited his signature. "Here's the pen."

Morgan's actions saved the day and the balances of most of his moneyed friends. Possibly they prevented the financial panic from triggering a general depression. For this he was feted as a hero. Even Roosevelt expressed his appreciation. But the capital-ist statesman could never stop thinking like a capitalist. At a cru-cial moment for the trust companies Morgan posed a question, which he proceeded to answer. "Why should I get into this? My affairs are all in order. I've done enough. I won't take all this on *unless I get what I want out of it.*"

What Morgan most wanted at this particular time was the cooperation of the federal government in a merger that would strengthen his steel trust. The fate of one Wall Street house hung on the value of the stock of the Tennessee Coal and Iron Company. Morgan proposed that U.S. Steel offer to purchase Tennessee Coal. The mere offer would boost the Tennessee shares and save its broker; the actual purchase would bolster the preeminence in the steel industry of U.S. Steel, and for this rea-son would have engaged the scrutiny of Roosevelt's Justice Department. Morgan sent two directors of U.S. Steel, Elbert Gary and Henry Frick, to Washington to discuss the matter with the president. Gary and Frick, poor-mouthing the prospects of

Tennessee Coal, presented the merger as their contribution to stemming the financial distress.

Roosevelt's grasp of politics had always been surer than his grip on finance, and the thought of sending his party into elections the following year amid a depression caused him to set aside his suspicions of Morgan. "I answered that while of course I could not advise them to take the action proposed," Roosevelt recorded after the meeting, "I felt it no public duty of mine to interpose any objection."

ONCE THE PANIC SUBSIDED, the sweetheart steel deal was what people remembered—that and the fact that once again Morgan had held the fate of American finance in his hand. Roosevelt retired from the White House to safari in Africa, prompting sighs of relief among the big capitalists. "May every lion do its part," Morgan was alleged to have said.

Perhaps he did say that, but if so he soon came to realize that worse than Roosevelt could befall the moneyed class. Roosevelt was the first progressive president—the first chief executive to believe that government should reclaim for democracy much of what the capitalists had seized during the decades of industrialization. But he wasn't the last. William Howard Taft continued Roosevelt's trust-busting, winning the most celebrated case of the era when his prosecutors broke up John D. Rockefeller's Standard Oil Company. And when Woodrow Wilson, the reforming governor of New Jersey, defeated Taft (and the back-from-Africa Roosevelt) in the 1912 election, the progressive handwriting was on the wall.

A principal complaint of the progressives was the power of the "money trust," by which they meant J. P. Morgan and his circle. "A few groups of financiers in the city of New York . . . have secured domination over many of the leading national banks and other moneyed institutions," the progressive majority in the House of Representatives declared. These groups sought "to control the money, exchange, security, and commodity markets . . . to the detriment of interstate commerce and of the general public." An investigation into the money trust was necessary and proper.

Morgan was supposed to be the star witness. No one knew more about money; no one possessed the moneyed power Morgan did. The investigative committee, headed by Democrat Arsène Pujo, prepared its questions carefully and enlisted the most able counsel it could find. The financial papers and the general press anticipated the interrogation with headline-writers ready.

But Morgan refused to cooperate. He resented the idea that his business should be revealed to the world, and he answered questions in the opaquest of terms. Samuel Untermyer, chief counsel for the committee, inquired about a transaction that appeared a patent case of chicanery, in which Morgan had paid $3 million for stock worth only $51,000 at par. Why had he done so?, Untermyer demanded.

"Because I thought it was a desirable thing," Morgan replied.

Untermyer rephrased the question.

Morgan reiterated: "I thought it was the thing to do."

"But that does not explain anything."

"That is the only reason I can give."

"It was the thing to do for whom?"

"That is the only reason I can give. That is the only reason I have, in other words. I am not trying to keep anything back, you understand."

"I understand. In other words, you have no reason at all."

"That is the way you look at it. I think it is a very good reason."

The guiding premise of the investigation was that a few powerful men enjoyed an operational monopoly of the money system in America. Morgan dismissed the idea as absurd. No one could get a monopoly of money.

Untermyer professed amazement. "There is no way one man can get a monopoly of money?"

"Or control of it," Morgan answered.

"He can make a try of it?"

"No, sir, he can not. He may have all the money in Christendom, but he can not do it."

"If you owned all the banks of New York, with all their resources, would you not come pretty near having a control of credit?"

"No, sir. Not at all."

Untermyer was mystified. "Is not the credit based upon the money?"

"No, sir."

"It has no relation?"

"No, sir."

What, then, was credit based on?, Untermyer asked.

"The first thing is character," Morgan answered.

"Before money or property?"

"Before money or anything else. Money can not buy it."

"So that a man with character, without anything at all behind it, can get all the credit he wants, and a man with the property can not get it?"

"That is very often the case. . . . I have known a man to come into my office, and I have given him a check for a million dollars when I knew they did not have a cent in the world."

The committee clearly didn't believe Morgan. The committee staff compiled a dossier on Morgan and the other big bankers, detailing the links among the financial institutions and between the banks and the railroads and industrial corporations. "J. P. Morgan & Co. of New York and Drexel & Co. of Philadelphia are one and the same firm," the Pujo report began. It proceeded to tally the directorships held by Morgan partners in Bankers Trust, Guaranty Trust, Astor Trust, the National Bank of Commerce, Chase National Bank, Chemical National Bank, Equitable Life Assurance, the New York Central Railroad, the Northern Pacific, U.S. Steel, International Harvester, General Electric, American Telephone and Telegraph, Western Union, and scores more companies, till the eyes of readers glazed over.

The report chided Morgan and other witnesses for refusing to cooperate in the investigation, but their recalcitrance only confirmed the committee's conclusion. "There is an established and well-defined identity and community of interest between a few leaders of finance, created and held together through stock ownership, interlocking directorates, partnership and joint account transactions, and other forms of domination over banks, trust companies, railroads, and public-service and industrial corporations, which has resulted in great and rapidly growing concentration of the control of money and credit in the hands of these few men." The committee didn't gainsay the constructive role the money men had played in the development of the American economy. "Without the aid of their invaluable enterprise and initiative and their credit and financial power, the money requirements of our vast ventures could not have been financed." But by eliminating competition and monopolizing access to money, the inner circle endangered democracy. "The peril is manifest."

Epilogue
The Money Answer

Morgan hadn't been well when the hearings began, and the strain of dueling with Untermyer and dealing with reporters wore him out. He was seventy-five years old and longed to escape from the cares of business. By annual habit he updated his will as 1913 began, and he set forth on a vacation cruise shortly after. One of his private steam yachts had gone ahead to the Nile, and the vessel carried Morgan and his party south to the temples at Luxor. The craft was as fast as any afloat—Morgan regularly traded up—but its progress failed to satisfy him. He grew increasingly, and uncharacteristically for him on holiday, impatient. He couldn't sleep and fell into a depression. The doctors he kept on retainer were summoned from New York, and the vacationers turned back down the Nile. They steamed to Italy, where the art dealers he had patronized for years prayed for his recovery. But his nervousness increased, his insomnia grew more intractable, and his heart raced and stuttered. He developed a fever from a cause the physicians couldn't

identify and took to bed at his usual suite in Rome's Grand
Hotel. He died on March 31.

Morgan's intimates were sure *they* knew the cause of the
death: Pujo and his inquisitors had done the great man in.
"Within three or four months," a Morgan partner recalled, "out of
a seemingly clear sky, his health failed and after a two weeks' illness, from no particular malady, he died." The frustrated doctors
agreed, with one declaring, "I wish Untermyer and the Pujo
Committee were where I would like them to be!"

The reading of the Morgan will surprised many of his contem-
poraries. His estate, exclusive of his art collection, amounted to
a mere $68 million. "And to think, he was not a rich man,"
mused Andrew Carnegie, who had personally pocketed $225
million from the sale of his steel business to Morgan's U.S. Steel
trust.

NO ONE QUITE knew it at the time, but Morgan's passing
marked the end of an age. The revelation of his comparative
penury made his money power all the more impressive, for it
showed what reputation and connections could do. And it doubled the resolve of the progressives to curtail the influence of
those money men who hankered to succeed Morgan. Within
months President Wilson went to Congress to demand legislation revamping the American money system. Proposals for a new
central bank had circulated since the Panic of 1907; the problem
was to determine whether it should be a private bank, like the
first and second Banks of the United States, or a public bank.

The bankers and most capitalists favored the former; as always they feared the baleful influence of democracy on the management of money. The progressives contended that democracy was the *only* solution to the nation's money woes; hadn't the recent investigations revealed that the capitalists regularly conspired against the public interest? Money was too important to be left to the money men.

The debate raged in the press, in the corridors of Congress, and in the saloons of Washington, but in the end something remarkable occurred. After twelve decades of bitter conflict between the capitalists and the democrats over the money question, the two camps reached a compromise. Their solution wasn't elegant; many thought it downright ugly. The Federal Reserve Act of 1913 created a hybrid system combining important elements of both capitalism and democracy. The twelve Federal Reserve banks were privately capitalized but answered to a board appointed by the White House. Gold remained the basis of the money supply, but the Federal Reserve Board, by manipulating interest rates and the reserve requirements of member banks, could strongly influence bank lending and thereby provide the "elastic currency" the drafters of the legislation agreed the country required.

Certain provisions of the act turned out to be more significant than the drafters or the debaters realized. The Reserve banks were empowered to buy and sell government securities; this power became the basis for fine-tuning the money supply. The board of governors was authorized to tax the Reserve banks to pay its operating expenses; this freed the board from dependence on Congress.

Both the capitalists and the democrats might have fretted
more about what they didn't get in the new system had greater
worries—and opportunities—not emerged within months. In
August 1914 Europe went to war. The capitalists soon began
floating loans to the belligerents, while the democrats—or most
of them, initially—tried to keep the war from sucking America
in. The democrats' avoidance strategy failed, not least because
the capitalists' lending strategy succeeded so well. By early 1917
the bankers had sent some $2.3 billion to Europe, with the over-
whelming majority of the money going to Britain and France,
which had stronger ties to Wall Street than Germany had (and
a more successful naval blockade of enemy ports). A defeat of
the British and French, whatever it might do to the balance of
military and moral power in Europe, would break the American
banks and likely ravage the American economy. Woodrow
Wilson was no cat's paw for the capitalists, but he couldn't
ignore reality, and his policies tilted increasingly toward Britain
and France, culminating in American intervention on their side
in April 1917.

The American war effort, besides securing the bankers' port-
folios, produced a revolution in federal finances. A new income
tax, authorized under the recent Sixteenth Amendment, was dramatically expanded during the war. Because the part of the
American workforce that received cash incomes had continued
to grow dramatically—by 1915 only about three workers out of
ten still toiled on farms—the modern income tax stood on a
much broader base than the Civil War version, and it allowed
what proved to be a permanent shift away from the tariff as the

primary source of government revenue. By war's end the tax rates
on the highest incomes reached 67 percent.

   The first serious test of the Federal Reserve system in its role
as arbiter of the nation's money occurred during the decade after
the war. The Fed lowered interest rates, in part to encourage
Europeans to invest at home, in order to reconstruct the plant
and infrastructure ravaged by the war. But the cheap money trig-
gered speculation, and a large bubble developed in the American
stock market. The Fed thereupon raised interest rates, yet not
enough to halt the speculation, which grew ever more frenzied
till the bubble burst in October 1929. As in previous panics,
money disappeared amid the crumbling of banks and the flight
of investors.

   At this point the Fed should have loosened the strings, but it
didn't. The democratically appointed governors as yet knew too
little about money and banking to realize what was required, and
the capitalists in the Reserve banks continued to think too much
like bankers to take the risk. The only person who might have
stepped Morgan-like into the breach had lately died. Benjamin
Strong had been president of Bankers Trust in Morgan's day and
had learned from the master the art of managing the nation's
money. After Morgan's passing he accepted appointment to head
the New York Federal Reserve Bank, where he wielded an influence that reflected both his own self-confidence and the first-
among-equals status of the New York bank. Strong was the one
who shaped the easy-money policy of the early 1920s and the
shift to greater stringency as the stock market soared. Strong
understood the potential of the Fed for dealing with financial

crises. "The very existence of the Federal Reserve System is a
safeguard against anything like a calamity growing out of money
rates," he wrote. "We have the power to deal with such an emergency instantly by flooding the Street with money." But Strong
died in 1928, and when the emergency he foresaw developed, no
one had the nerve to open the sluice gates. The Fed kept interest
rates high, with the result that the American money supply contracted by a strangling one-third.

The Fed wasn't alone in fumbling policy as the Great Crash
became the Great Depression. Congress and Herbert Hoover
collaborated to raise taxes and reduce spending, on the reasoning
that government should tighten its belt along with everyone else,
when lower taxes and higher spending would have helped pull
the economy out of its downward spiral. Congress raised tariff
rates, and Hoover approved them, in the hope of preserving the
home market for domestic producers. But the tariff increase
encouraged foreign countries to retaliate, sparking a trade war
that beggared the entire Atlantic neighborhood.

The international aspect of the depression was what drove
Franklin Roosevelt to implement the dream of William Jennings
Bryan. The depression forced Britain off the gold standard in
1931; the consequent devaluation of the British pound gave
Britain a competitive advantage in trade with other countries.
Roosevelt refused to cede the market without a fight and in 1933
suspended redemption of dollars by gold, effectively taking the
United States off the gold standard. Congress ratified his deci-
sion several months later, consigning gold to the dustbin of
American monetary history. Gold would make an international

comeback at the end of World War II, but for America's domestic purposes it ceased to exist as money at the beginning of 1934. The call of Bryan for silver had never been so much about silver as about gold; by nixing gold Roosevelt and the New Deal Congress finally gave the aurophobes what they wanted.

In doing so they left the country more reliant on the Fed than ever. The central bank learned from the depression and never repeated its deflationary mistake. During the following decades it occasionally erred in the opposite direction, doing too little in the 1960s and 1970s to counteract the inflationary triple whammy of Great Society social spending, Vietnam War military spending, and OPEC-extorted energy spending. (It was during the early 1970s that Richard Nixon took the United States off the international gold standard, thereby completing Roosevelt's Bryanic work.) But behind the leadership of Paul Volcker, the Fed in the 1980s eased the economy to a soft landing. And under Volcker's successor, Alan Greenspan, the Fed acted with dispatch and verve after a stock market crash in October 1987, flooding the markets with the cash Benjamin Strong had prescribed for such an event in the 1920s and preventing the stock swoon from becoming a general swan dive.

The economic boom of the 1990s made Greenspan a capitalist hero and then a political icon. Presidents of both parties basked in his celebrity. The bursting of the tech bubble at the beginning of the twenty-first century dimmed the Greenspan glow somewhat, but again the Fed kept the woes of the stock market from depressing the larger economy. The millennium recession was, by long-term historical standards, shallow and brief.

By those same historical standards, such debates as the recession evoked were polite and subdued, which underscored how completely the money question had vanished from American politics. The passion that had fueled the fight over Alexander Hamilton's Bank of the United States, that had driven Andrew Jackson and Nicholas Biddle to mortal combat over the second Bank, that had caused the Treasury Department to stiff Jay Cooke even as the Union depended on the bonds he sold, that had surrounded Jay Gould's raid on the nation's gold supply, that had made J. P. Morgan the most feared, hated, and indispensable man in America, had gone into other issues. The capitalists and the democrats still fought, but no longer over money per se. The ceasefire they achieved with the creation of the Federal Reserve held firm, nine decades after their heavy artillery and sniping rifles fell silent.

Money men still prowled the political economy, seeking their own interest and sometimes the nation's. A few, like Greenspan, became household names. But with the money question long since answered—as fully, at any rate, as it was likely to be answered in America—they lacked the notoriety and in nearly all cases the influence of the giants of the past. Money policy was far more successful than when those giants had battled, but it was also far less entertaining.

Notes

1: The Aristocracy of Capital

Page 19: "I contemn": Alexander Hamilton, *Writings*, ed. Joanne B. Freeman (2001), 3.

19: "I am a good deal puzzled": ibid., 5.

20: "Good God!": ibid., 6–9.

20: "That Americans": ibid., 11, 20.

21: "personal dependence": Forrest McDonald, *Alexander Hamilton* (1979), 14.

22: "I noticed a youth": Richard Brookhiser, *Alexander Hamilton* (1999), 28.

22: "Folly, caprice": *Writings*, 48–50.

23: "She must be young": ibid., 60.

25: "The fundamental defect": ibid., 70–83.

27: "It was the most affecting": ibid., 90.

27: "For three years": ibid., 94–95.

28: "Proposals of accommodation": ibid., 97.

29: "A WANT OF POWER": ibid., 99, 108, 118.

30: "He always comes": Brookhiser, 53.

30: "I have myself": *Writings*, 125–26.

31: "to devise such further": ibid., 144.

33: "most fatal . . . set fire to": H. W. Brands, *The First American* (2000), 670–71.

33: "The present system": ibid., 672.

34: "unfriendly . . . fondness for democracies": *Writings,* 151–58; Max Farrand, ed., *The Records of the Federal Convention of 1787* (1923), 1:299–300.

35: "If you will": *Records,* 3:85.

35: "I am seriously": ibid., 166-67.

36: "commercial interest": ibid., 167–68.

36: "A man must be far gone . . . awful spectacle": *The Federalist* (1788), nos. 6, 7, 11, 30, 85 (in *Writings* and many other places).

38: "The vast continent . . . fruits of it": Brands, *First American,* 693.

39: "the disrepute of having": *Writings,* 513.

39: "national blessing . . . price of liberty": *Writings,* 531ff.

44: "My soul arises . . . minister forever": Ron Chernow, *Alexander Hamilton* (2004), 303.

46: "clever man": Jack N. Rakove, *James Madison and the Creation of the American Republic* (1990), 88.

46: "Credit is an *entire thing*": Chernow, 302.

48: "This is the real history": Dumas Malone, *Jefferson and the Rights of Man* (1951), 301.

48: "not only as an ordinary bank": Smith, *Wealth of Nations* (1776) bk. 2, chap. 2, para. 85.

49: "Such a Bank . . . to the United States": *Writings,* 575ff.

53: "What was it drove": M. St. Clair Clarke and D. A. Hall, *Legislative and Documentary History of the Bank of the United States* (1832), 55–56.

53: "was condemned": ibid., 44–45.

54: "A little difference": ibid., 93–94.

54: "This *general principle*": *Writings,* 613–14.

55: Thirty members of Congress: Bray Hammond, *Banks and Politics in America* (1957), 123.

2. The Bank War

Page 58: "Me thought": David McCullough, *John Adams* (2001), 469.

60: "There are great and intrinsic defects": Alexander Hamilton, *Writings,* ed. Joanne B. Freeman (2001), 935, 970.

61: "The violence of party": *The Correspondence of Nicholas Biddle,* ed. Reginald C. McGrane (1919), 3–4.

62: "Every good citizen": Thomas Payne Govan, *Nicholas Biddle* (1959), 18.

63: "Is this a time": ibid., 34.

63: "This Bank is to begin": M. St. Clair Clarke and D. A. Hall, *Legislative and Documentary History of the Bank of the United States* (1832), 567.

64: "That it has been perverted": *Correspondence of Biddle,* 12.

65: "I am unwilling": ibid.

66: from $22 million: Murray N. Rothbard, *The Panic of 1819* (1962), 12.

66: "distress . . . or shoes": Samuel Rezneck, "The Depression of 1819–1822," *American Historical Review* 39 (1933): 30.

67: "Let the end be legitimate . . . dependent on the states": Kermit L. Hall, ed., *The Oxford Companion to the Supreme Court* (1992), 536–38.

68: "talent for business": *Correspondence of Biddle,* 27–28.

69: "I prefer my last letters": ibid., 81–82.

71: "There is no one principle": *Correspondence of Biddle,* 62–63.

72: Jackson's first annual message: *Messages and Papers of the Presidents,* comp. James D. Richardson (1917), 3:1025.

73: "They should be treated": *Correspondence of Biddle,* 91.

74: "referred to the people": ibid., 112–13.

75: "In respect to General Jackson": ibid., 122.

75: "real and positive information": ibid., 123–24.

75: "I believe my retainer": ibid., 218.

76: "My own belief": ibid., 142.

76: "great and beneficent institution": H. W. Brands, *Andrew Jackson* (2005), 463.

77: "We have determined": *Correspondence of Biddle,* 161–63.

77: "connected intimately": *Register of Debates,* 22nd Congress, 1st session (Senate), 54.

78: "A disordered currency": Thomas Hart Benton, *Thirty Years' View* (1854), 1:244.

79: "They lead to the *abduction*": *Register of Debates,* 22:1 (Senate), 139–41.

80: "I do not mean": Arthur M. Schlesinger Jr., *The Age of Jackson* (1945), 87.

81: "A bank of the United States": *Messages and Papers,* 3:1139–54.

83: "A more deranging": George Rogers Taylor, ed., *Jackson vs. Biddle's Bank* (1972), 30–33.

84: "astonishment, indignation, and alarm": ibid.

84: "I am delighted": *Correspondence of Biddle,* 196.

84: "The veto works well": *Correspondence of Andrew Jackson,* ed. John Spencer Bassett (1926–35), 4:467.

85: "They will not *dare*": ibid., 202.

85: "This operation": *Correspondence of Jackson,* 5:22–23.

86: "Most of the banks": ibid., 5:146, 169–70.

86: "The real sin": *Correspondence of Biddle,* 209–10.

87: "The mass of the people": *Correspondence of Jackson,* 5:192–203.

88: "It is dreadful here": *Correspondence of Biddle,* 217–18.

89: "My view is simply this": ibid., 219–20.

89: "The future is full": ibid., 221–22.

90: "My conscience told me": *Correspondence of Jackson,* 5:217, 238.

90: "There is no real general distress . . . were put down": ibid., 5:244.

91: "Relief, sir!": Ralph C. H. Catterall, *The Second Bank of the United States* (1902, 1960), 351–52; James Parton, *Life of Andrew Jackson* (1860–61), 3:549–50.

91: "The Bank, Mr. Van Buren": *The Autobiography of Martin Van Buren,* ed. John C. Fitzpatrick (1920), 625.

92: "There is one cause": Catterall, 357.

92: "You will of course": *Correspondence of Biddle,* 251–52.

92: "gang of banditti": ibid., 255.

93: "It transferred specie": Bray Hammond, *Banks and Politics in America* (1957), 456.

94: "The crusade against banks": ibid., 461.

94: "Looking out": Charles Dickens, *American Notes* (1874), 112–13.

3. The Bonds of Union

Page 99: "heart-broken": Thomas Payne Govan, *Nicholas Biddle* (1959), 411.

102: "With lightning rapidity": Ellis Paxson Oberholtzer, *Jay Cooke* (1907), 1:69–70.

103: "Our firm": ibid., 81–83.

104: "Money is not *tight*": Henrietta M. Larson, *Jay Cooke* (1936, 1968), 80; Meade Minnigerode, *Certain Rich Men* (1927), 58.

104: "The subscribers": Larson, 107–8.

105: "It is regarded": ibid., 111.

106: "There is nothing . . . possessed them": James M. McPherson, *Battle Cry of Freedom* (1988), 344–45.

107: "Toombs never": Oberholtzer, 1:124–25.

109: "The wit of man . . . very purpose": McPherson, 446.

110: "I am pained": Oberholtzer, 1:173.

110: "Immediate action": *Congressional Globe*, 37th Congress, 2nd session, 618.

112: seventy-five percent: Paul Studenski and Herman E. Krooss, *Financial History of the United States* (1952, 1963), 148.

112: "Can't you sell": Larson, 102–3.

112: "I have talked": ibid., 108.

113: "It is an office": Oberholtzer, 1:137.

114: "I hope": Bray Hammond, *Sovereignty and an Empty Purse* (1970), 82.

115: "Mr. Chase": Oberholtzer, 1:152.

115: "Kate Chase . . . and house": ibid., 154–55.

116: "We can do the work": Larson, 115.

117: "TO FARMERS": Oberholtzer, 1:252.

118: "1st. Why are they called": ibid., 238–40.

120: "A Day at the Agency": ibid., 242–43.

121: "Poor fellow": ibid., 231.

121: nearly $2.5 million: Larson, 144.

122: "Mr. Lincoln": Oberholtzer, 1:200–201.

123: "Notes were printed": ibid., 327.

124: "There can be": Bray Hammond, *Banks and Politics in America* (1957), 727.

124: "Seeing that he . . . warm support": Oberholtzer, 1:331–34.

126: "I have constantly": Larson, 149.

126: "Some passages . . . sure of it": ibid., 165–69.

128: "The fame of Jay Cooke": Oberholtzer, 1:573–74; Minnigerode, 62.

129: "The Yankees": Oberholtzer, 1:574.

4. The Great Gold Conspiracy

Page 134: "When intensely interested": H. W. Brands, *Masters of Enterprise* (1999), 39.

135: "Along with the ordinary": ibid., 40.

136: "Daniel says up": Meade Minnigerode, *Certain Rich Men* (1927), 85.

137: "If this printing press": Brands, *Masters,* 24.

137: "Their only chance": Charles Francis Adams Jr. and Henry Adams, *Chapters of Erie* (1886, 1956), 29–30.

139: "a cavern full . . . to eat": Brands, *Masters,* 41–42.

141: "Business got very dull": U.S. House of Representatives, Committee on Banking and Commerce, *Investigation into the Causes of the Gold Panic* (1870), 132.

141: "How will the rise . . . really buying": ibid., 131–32.

144: "I supposed . . . the President": ibid., 133, 151–52.

145: "He was our guest . . . not look promising": ibid., 152–54, 172–73.

146: "At a time of the year": *New York Times,* Aug. 25, 1869.

146: "The President": *Investigation,* 153.

147: "that Mrs. Grant": ibid., 173.

147: "I did not want": ibid., 135–36.

149: "I was told . . . ALL RIGHT": ibid., 9, 444.

150: "He figured . . . letter gets out": ibid., 157, 256.

151: "The bear party": *New York Times,* Sept. 24, 1869.

152: "I had my own": *Investigation,* 141.

153: "practical *corner*": ibid., 279.

153: "Take all . . . at 160": ibid., 65.

154: "If gold advanced": ibid., 344.

155: "Gold over": ibid., 345–46.

156: "Amid all the noise": ibid., 37–38.

157: "the chances were": Brands, *Masters,* 47.

158: "Nothing is lost": Matthew Josephson, *The Robber Barons* (1934, 1995), 141.

158: "He has no courage": Maury Klein, *The Life and Legend of Jay Gould* (1986), 113.

158: "It was each man": *Investigation,* 176.

5. The Transit of Jupiter

Page 159 "There was no sorrow": H. W. Brands, *Masters of Enterprise* (1999), 49.

160: "to keep things steady": Ellis Paxson Oberholtzer, *Jay Cooke* (1907), 2:143.

160: "I have been writing": Henrietta M. Larson, *Jay Cooke* (1936, 1968), 270–71.

162: "Owing to unexpected demands": Oberholtzer, 2:424.

162: "A thunderclap": ibid., 422–23, 432–33.

163: "The banker's calling": Ron Chernow, *The House of Morgan* (1991), 20.

165: "I will agree": Herbert L. Satterlee, *J. Pierpont Morgan* (1939), 226.

165: "The purpose": George Wheeler, *Pierpont Morgan and Friends* (1973), 178.

166: "RAILROAD KINGS": Maury Klein, *The Life and Legend of Jay Gould* (1986), 460.

166: "Men died": Henry Adams, *The Education of Henry Adams* (1906, 1961), 338.

167: "Never before . . . for law": Robert Sobel, *Panic on Wall Street* (1968, 1988), 260.

167: "school of finance": William H. Harvey, *Coin's Financial School* (1895; ed. Richard Hofstadter, 1963), 93–95.

168: "In money": ibid., 95–99.

169: "silent tread of a cat": ibid., 105–9.

169: "The value . . . gold standard": ibid., 188, 191, 194, 195.

170: "It is commonly . . . by man": ibid., 204, 211, 221–22.

172: "Give the people": ibid., 233–38.

175: "In the struggle": ibid., 239.

176: "I have been dreadfully": *Letters of Grover Cleveland*, ed. Allan Nevins (1933), 376.

177: "I have come . . . has been reached": Satterlee, 286–92.

179: "That I decline": ibid., 318.

180: "their dead": H. W. Brands, *The Reckless Decade* (1995), 255.

180: "The silver men . . . 16 to 1": ibid., 257–58.

181: "The humblest citizen": Richard Hofstadter and Beatrice Hofstadter, *Great Issues in American History* (1982), 3:158.

181: "At the close": Brands, *Reckless Decade*, 259.

182: "We reply . . . cross of gold": Hofstadter and Hofstadter, 3:160–65.

185: "God's in his heaven": Brands, *Reckless Decade*, 286.

186: "Don't any of you realize": H. W. Brands, *TR* (1997), 397.

187: "If we have done": ibid., 437.

189: "The Secretary": *New York Times*, Oct. 23, 1907.

189: "If he could not": Satterlee, 467.

189: "There goes . . . *hour today!*": ibid., 473–74.

191: "If people": ibid., 476.

192: "Here's the place": Sobel, 320.

193: "I answered": Brands, *TR,* 603.

194: "A few groups": H.R. 504, Apr. 22, 1912, in *Report of the Committee Appointed Pursuant to House Resolutions 429 and 504 to Investigate the Concentration of Control of Money and Credit* (1913), 175–76.

194: "Because I thought . . . good reason": ibid., 83–84.

195: "There is no way . . . in the world": ibid., 136; Chernow, 154.

196: "There is an established": *Report,* 129, 140, 159.

Epilogue: The Money Answer

Page 200: "Within three or four months": Ron Chernow, *The House of Morgan* (1991), 158.

200: "I wish Untermyer": Jean Strouse, *Morgan* (1999), 678.

200: "And to think": ibid., 159.

201: "elastic currency": 38 Stat. 251 (Dec. 23, 1913).

204: "The very existence": John Steele Gordon, *Hamilton's Blessing* (1997), 116–17.

For Further Reading

Of the individuals profiled here, Alexander Hamilton has received the greatest attention. The most recent and perhaps the best overall treatment of Hamilton's life and career is Ron Chernow, *Alexander Hamilton* (2004), although Richard Brookhiser's much shorter *Alexander Hamilton, American* (1999) runs a close second. John Steele Gordon starts with Hamilton to examine the rise and fall and rise and rise of the national debt in *Hamilton's Blessing: The Extraordinary Life and Times of Our National Debt* (1997).

Nicholas Biddle has rated a single full biography: Thomas Payne Govan, *Nicholas Biddle: Nationalist and Public Banker, 1786–1844* (1959). But his fight with Andrew Jackson over the Bank of the United States figures in every creditable account of Jackson's presidency, including Robert V. Remini, *Andrew Jackson,* volumes 2 and 3 (1981, 1984), and H. W. Brands, *Andrew Jackson: His Life and Times* (2005).

Jay Cooke is handled in full and friendly fashion in Ellis

Paxson Oberholzer, *Jay Cooke: Financier of the Civil War*, 2 volumes (1905; 1968 reprint), and Henrietta M. Larson, *Jay Cooke:
Private Banker* (1936; 1968 reprint). His railroad ventures are
described in John L. Harnsberger, *Jay Cooke and Minnesota: The
Formative Years of the Northern Pacific Railroad, 1868–1873*
(1981), and the forthcoming M. John Lubetkin, *Jay Cooke's
Gamble: The Northern Pacific Railroad, the Sioux, and the Panic
of 1873* (2006).

Jay Gould couldn't catch a break from biographers and histori-
ans till Maury Klein came to his rescue with *The Life and Legend
of Jay Gould* (1987). Since then Gould has fascinated Kenneth D.
Ackerman, who wrote *The Gold Ring: Jim Fisk, Jay Gould, and
Black Friday, 1869* (1988), and Charles R. Morris, author of
*Tycoons: How Andrew Carnegie, John D. Rockefeller, Jay Gould,
and J. P. Morgan Invented the American Supereconomy* (2005). An
earlier account of Gould's ilk, whose pages still smoke from the
author's ire, is Matthew Josephson, *The Robber Barons: The Great
American Capitalists, 1861–1901* (1934; 1995 reprint). Almost as
entertaining is John Steele Gordon, *The Scarlet Woman of Wall
Street: Jay Gould, Jim Fisk, Cornelius Vanderbilt, the Erie Railway
Wars, and the Birth of Wall Street* (1988).

J. P. Morgan is often treated as part of his dynasty. Of such
treatments the most insightful is Ron Chernow, *The House of
Morgan: An American Banking Dynasty and the Rise of Modern
Finance* (1990). Of the biographical works, the place to start is
Jean Strouse, *Morgan: American Financier* (1999). Andrew
Sinclair, *Corsair: The Life of J. Pierpont Morgan* (1981), is brisker.

Written histories of money and finance are often dated or dull.

Bray Hammond, *Banks and Politics in America, from the Revolution to the Civil War* (1957) and *Sovereignty and an Empty Purse: Banks and Politics in the Civil War* (1970), are a bit of both, but still the best works on their subjects. Ralph C. H. Catterall, *The Second Bank of the United States* (1902; 1960 reprint), is definitely both, but the best on *its* subject. Edward S. Kaplan, *The Bank of the United States and the American Economy* (1999), is less weighty in content and tone. More specialized are Susan Hoffmann, *Politics and Banking: Ideas, Public Policy, and the Creation of Financial Institutions* (2001), and Howard Bodenhorn, *State Banking in Early America: A New Economic History* (2003). Robert E. Wright, *The First Wall Street: Chestnut Street, Philadelphia, and the Birth of American Finance* (2005), gives America's original financial hub its due. The first part of James Grant, *Money of the Mind: Borrowing and Lending in America from the Civil War to Michael Milken* (1992), covers the last part of the present book.

The emergence and operation of the Federal Reserve can be followed in James Livingston, *Origins of the Federal Reserve System: Money, Class, and Corporate Capitalism, 1890 to 1913* (1986), and Bernard Shull, *The Fourth Branch: The Federal Reserve's Unlikely Rise to Power and Influence* (2005). William Greider's powerful and provocative *Secrets of the Temple: How the Federal Reserve Runs the Country* (1987), is in a class by itself.

Panics in the financial markets are always entertaining (to read about); they receive their due in Robert Sobel, *Panic on Wall Street: A Classic History of America's Financial Disasters with*

a New Exploration of the Crash of 1987 (1988), and Elmus
Wicker, *Banking Panics of the Gilded Age* (2000).

Wall Street's story is told in Charles R. Geisst, *Wall Street: A
History* (1997), and Steven Fraser, *Every Man a Speculator: A
History of Wall Street in American Life* (2005).

Acknowledgments

The author would like to thank James Atlas and Jesse Cohen of Atlas Books, Ed Barber of W. W. Norton, and James D. Hornfischer of Hornfischer Literary Management. Special thanks to Amy Robbins for a fine copyediting job.

Index

Page numbers in *italics* refer to illustrations.